Dear Selma and Hal,
My dear friends.
To happy memories!
With love,
Estelle

ITZIK & MICKEY
Stories from Brooklyn & Beyond

Itzik

Mickey

ITZIK & MICKEY
Stories from Brooklyn & Beyond

by

Irving (Itzik) Glasser &

Myron (Mickey) Glazer

Introductions by
Paul Glasser & Josh Glazer

Copyright © 2014 Myron Glazer

All rights reserved including the right of reproduction in whole or in part in any form.

Off the Common Books · Amherst, Massachusetts

ISBN 978-1-937146-67-2

Printed in the United States of America

for ESTELLE

and for PENINA

with love

Table of Contents

PREFACE (MG)	ix
IT WASN'T SO GREAT: INTRODUCTION TO ITZIK By Paul Glasser	xiii
A PLENTIFUL BOUNTY: INTRODUCTION TO MICKEY By Josh Glazer	xix

PART I – WELCOME TO EAST NEW YORK

1.	443 HEGEMAN AVENUE (IG)	1
2.	RIDING INTO THE SUNSET (MG)	6

PART II – FAMILY FOREVER

3.	MY SISTER THE MONSTER (IG)	13
4.	FINDING JERRY (MG)	19
5.	CHOCOLATE PUDDING (IG)	25

PART III – WORKERS AND ENTREPRENEURS

6.	AN ARRESTING EXPERIENCE (IG)	35
	THE SODA KID (IG)	38
	THE APPLE OF MY EYE (MG)	44
9.	MY MOTHER NEVER WORKED (IG)	52

PART IV – OLD FRIENDS AND GOOD PEOPLE

10.	MRS. YOUSHAK (IG)	59
11.	JUST AN ORDINARY MAN (MG)	67
12.	IN THE BEST OF COMPANY (MG)	69

Table of Contents continued

PART V – FACING OUR DEMONS
13. THE CELLAR (IG)   79
14. DINNER FOR FOUR IN PARIS (MG)   85

PART VI – DANGEROUS JOURNEYS
15. GOING TO THE COUNTRY (IG)   97
16. A PUBLIC AND PRIVATE NUISANCE (MG)   102

PART VII – A NEW IDENTITY
17. FALLING OUT OF LOVE (MG)   113
18. MY FIRST REAL JOB (IG)   119

PART VIII – FALLING IN LOVE
19. THIS IS YOUR LIFE, ESTELLE WYETZNER (IG)   127
20. KISSING AGAIN (MG)   131
21. THE GIRL WITH THE FUNNY NAME (MG)   139

PART IX – IN MEMORIAM
22. MY SISTER, MY TEACHER (MG)   145
23. THE SUMMER OF 1967 (MG)   149
24. APPROPOS OF NOTHING: AN APPRECIATION   153
    By Danny Glasser

ACKNOWLEDGMENTS   157

ABOUT THE AUTHORS   158

Preface

Mickey Glazer

My brother Itzik died in June 1994. He was just shy of his sixty-ninth birthday, and he left behind a treasure trove of humorous and poignant stories. Itz was nine years older than I and he had always been my hero. As a child I longed to join him on the streets of our neighborhood in East New York/Brownsville, where he excelled as a punchball athlete. He could out-punch, out-catch, and out-run all of his friends. He repeatedly told me that he looked forward to the day when I would be old enough and skilled enough to compete with the boys from Hegeman Avenue. Happily, the time did come when I was invited to play on Itz's team. To make up for my deficiencies in height and strength, the opposing team agreed never to hit the ball directly at me, and that worked out fine for a seven-year-old kid. If the play was too difficult for me, Itz was always there to cover and make sure I did not misplay the ball.

Itz served in the army during World War II, from 1943 through 1946. When he returned from the war, I was eleven years old. Under the GI Bill he began to take writing courses, hoping that he could hone his skills and become a comedy writer for one or more of the contemporary comedians. As he perfected his various routines over the years—first for radio and then for television stars—he would adopt the persona of the comedian in question. Some days he would walk around our apartment in the guise of Groucho Marx; other times he became Sid Caesar or Howard Morris. His friends and family loved his routines, but commercial acceptance evaded him. Over time, his goals changed. He began taking different creative writing courses at Brooklyn College. They led him to build a body of work documenting life in Brooklyn during the Great Depression. His stories were bittersweet depictions of poverty and resilience. He could make us laugh even when recalling our family's constant moves from one apartment to another because there was not enough money for rent. We were either dispossessed (the Depression term for "evicted") or tempted by another landlord's concessions for three months of free rent. Itz captured the humiliation he felt wearing hand-me-down clothes from begrudging relatives, while admiring my mother's skill in patching and starching and ironing old clothes so her four children looked respectable.

With Itz's untimely death, we no longer heard a new story at every family party and event. Occasionally, his wife Estelle or one of his children would retrieve one of the classics and read it on his birthday. But in the main the stories were stored away in cartons awaiting some final distribution. We all knew that we wanted to protect the stories for future generations but were unsure how to proceed.

Fate intervened in the person of Dorothy Goldstone, who offered a writing workshop on "Growing Up Jewish" at my Northampton synagogue. I had no intention of joining this workshop, but my wife Penina persuaded me that I should try it. I had written many articles and books on academic subjects, but I had never done personal essay writing of any kind. With Dorothy's encouragement and the support of my fellow workshop participants, I soon found myself fully engaged in writing about my life. Some of the stories reflected on my childhood in Brooklyn, but others covered events that spanned my adult years.

As I developed this collection of stories an idea began to form: What if we took some of Itz's best work and combined it with the stories I was writing to produce a volume for all our grandchildren, family, and friends? And so this book was born. What was once an abstract dream became a reality with the assistance of Itz's children, Paul, Ruth, and Danny, who helped us collect and edit his stories. Paul wrote an introduction to his father's work, and my son Josh created an essay to introduce my stories.

The collection reveals an overlap of experience that permeates much of our writing. We both loved the radio heroes that we listened to every week—Tom Mix, the Lone Ranger, the Shadow, and more. We both shared a passion for baseball and a sense of humor that bound us together for all of our lives. But in some ways the fact that I was nine years younger created a gap in our experiences; we grew up in substantially different times. For Itz, the Glazers were never far from the throes of poverty, and he always believed he had to stand on constant guard against disaster that might befall the family. By comparison, I came of age when my family's economic circumstances were improved, after World War II, and I was able to leave Brooklyn to seek out a different kind of life. My siblings always felt that I was less burdened by the heavy cloak of childhood poverty and more able to take risks in building my future.

The stories in this collection are a constant reminder of struggles and obstacles in our lives, but there are equally potent themes of courage and caring. Life in the special culture of Brooklyn of the 1930s and '40s is long gone, but the legacy of those days lives on. Even today, I remember my brother's voice, reminding me that there is humor to be found in every situation. This is a legacy to be cherished and nourished, because with humor there is also hope. I have just spent several months reading and rereading my brother's stories—selecting the ones that best capture his pointed use of a small anecdote to reveal a larger picture. To a marked degree our stories reinforce and enrich each other. Bringing our writings together in a volume that will preserve them for posterity has been a great joy for me. I know the readers will share some of my pleasure.

Itz – the record salesman and prankster

It Wasn't So Great: Growing Up in the 1930s

Introduction by Paul Glasser

My father, Irving—Itzik—Glasser, was exceptionally talented. While he may never have been able to earn a living from his jokes and stories, they made a deep impression on everyone who knew him. He could spot people's foibles and caricature them better than most. In his short stories he manages to draw out both the humor and the pathos from a very traumatic era.

More than anyone else I know, my father was a child of the Great Depression, which, as he sarcastically noted over fifty years later, "really wasn't so great." Even his sisters and brother, who grew up in the same household, were less affected than he: the older of his two sisters, born in 1921, and the younger of the two, born in 1922, recall the somewhat better economic times the family enjoyed in the 1920s; his brother, born in 1934, remembers only as far back as the better times that came with the beginning of World War II.

My father, born in 1925, remembered back to the early 1930s, when the Depression was at its worst, and those memories shaped his entire life. His generation, or rather his fraction of a generation, could never be thrifty enough. To the end of his life, he could never clip enough supermarket coupons or refrain from buying on sale. Even when he no longer needed the money, and when it seemed that his time might be worth more than the money he saved, thriftiness came first—he remembered the days when a few pennies were worth far more than the time and effort necessary to save them.

My father always made sure that we children understood the value of money. Everything had to be earned. When we became old enough to have spending money, we were generally asked to help him or my mother around the house in exchange, and if we wanted any extra, he insisted that we work for it.

Even more than in his continued thriftiness, it was in his storytelling that my father's Depression upbringing manifested itself. Tale after tale revolved around the need to scrimp and save, the need to earn, the joy that came from saving a few pennies and then spending them with the greatest of caution. As my brother, Danny, said in the eulogy he composed, our father took the greatest pleasure in the little things in life, and his stories make it clear that he had always been like that. His telling how he was able to save up twenty-seven cents for a day with lunch and the movies seemed almost prehistoric to us—how could we imagine that those few pennies could be worth so much? (The same outing today would be approximately fifty times as expensive.) He told of collecting used bottles for the deposits. In an age when the five-cent deposit collected is laughable, how could we fathom the value of a two-cent deposit?

But more important than the direct significance of money was his keen eye for its effect on people's relations. His story "My Mother Never Worked," a sardonic description of my grandmother's daily routine, is almost shocking in its powerful appraisal of the backbreaking effort required to keep house when there was so little money available to the household and so few conveniences to reduce the housewife's labor. Not only did virtually everything have to be done by hand, but the amount of recycling, resewing, and restoring that my grandmother did is nearly beyond our comprehension today, when restaurant meals are frequent and slight damage to a garment is occasion for its being replaced. Moreover, the title of the story is a paraphrase of my grandfather's petulant dismissal of the value of housework—after all, my grandmother did not earn any money, and he did. The fact that she saved an untold amount with her skill and efficiency did not enter into my grandfather's balance sheet.

The additional fact that my grandfather, who owned a printing shop and refused to even consider employment in someone else's business, was unable to provide for the family doubtless increased his criticism of my grandmother, who was, after all, eminently successful in her profession. His attachment to his printing shop also caused resentment on the part of his children. They believed even a low-paying job for their father could have meant a steady income for the family, whereas the printing shop meant never knowing where the next dollar was coming from. Itzik and his sisters also resented the welfare (then known as "relief") bureaucracy that denied the family financial aid, because businessmen, however unsuccessful, were not considered needy and, obviously, not eligible for any cash payments or unemployment benefits. It's no wonder that my father looked over his shoulder frequently, even if half in jest, to assure himself that financial ruin was not gaining on him.

The silver lining to all this was that, in contrast to the lack of money, there was no shortage of family and friends. My father frequently recalled with great fondness the memories of playing all the typical New York street games with every other kid in Brownsville and East New York. He took immense pleasure in family get-togethers, and every new baby that arrived, whether his own or someone else's, was an occasion for rejoicing, as well as nearly smothering the child with affection. And although as a child I hated my father's teasing, looking back, it seems unfair to complain, since his rather gentle barbs were directly at everyone equally, including himself. Everyone and everything was fair game. The slightest slip-up, observed by my father, might earn you a reputation for your whole life. Decades after an incident took place, it would reemerge in conversation and you would find yourself the butt of his jokes again. But he knew where to draw the line. For example, when one relative began to become chubby, he teased her about her weight, but when she became truly fat, the joking ceased immediately. He joked repeatedly about his bald crown; for example, when the Mohawk haircut, with the head shaved except for the very top, was in fashion, he boasted that he had a "reverse Mohawk." But when someone thoughtlessly called him "Baldy," he was not above responding in kind, for he considered that remark to be unfair and unfunny.

While "irrepressible" was not the descriptor that I would have chosen, when my cousin David used it at my father's funeral it seemed more appropriate than I could have imagined. Having seen Dad every day, with his constant aches and pains and frequent fatigue, it did not seem to be the right word. But before larger groups of people, his true nature revealed itself— more than it did when it was just the five of us—and "irrepressible" seems just right.

Of course, he was incapable of repressing a joke, practical or otherwise. Sometimes I wished that he would joke around a little less, although I certainly knew his serious side. And his practical jokes were, mercifully, not the stupid, trite kind. No, they were unbelievably original. Just compiling them would be a huge job. Let's try to find a few.

There was the time I was introduced to Mozart's, "Eine Kleine Nachtmusik," which is probably the first classical piece I ever heard. "Now, what do you think Mozart's first name was?" he asked me, then four years old, "Wolfgang Amadeus, or Harold?" Well, I reasoned, it must be Harold, because nobody could have a name as ridiculous as Wolfgang Amadeus! And so I went around for several years thinking how beautiful Harold Mozart's music was.

Then there was the time he offered his nephew David a box of chocolate lollipops if he could get his father Terry, a great comedian, to be a straight man. David was supposed to get Terry to fall for the oldest joke in the book: "Daddy, my friend and I helped an old lady across the street today!" "Why did it take two of you?" "Because she didn't want to go...." David was three years old at the time and he loved those lollipops. So when Terry came home from work that day, David marched up to him and announced, "Daddy, my friend and I helped an old lady across the street today!" Almost before he finished the sentence, Terry exploded with a humorless, "Who said you were allowed to cross the street?" at which point David burst into tears, since he had lost his box of lollipops. Of course, Dad gave him the lollipops anyway. Moral of the story: not every comedian is a born straight man.

But not only children were the butt of my father's (almost) harmless practical joking. In the record store where he worked for several years in the '50s, he would do the same sorts of things to his customers. I've always wondered how he managed to hold a job, with some of the pranks he pulled! Like the time someone asked whether the store had a recording of "Oedipus Rex" in stock. "Certainly not!" he almost bellowed. The poor customer was taken aback. "Why not?" he inquired meekly. "Because when we heard he killed his father and married his mother, we wanted to have nothing to do with him!"

Or the time he was working near the United Nations and an unsuspecting Italian diplomat came in and asked for a certain recording by Enrico Caruso. The record happened to be out of stock, but Dad felt a joke coming on...and he was, after all, irrepressible. "I'm sorry, we don't have that record." "Why not?" "Because Caruso's dead." "But what difference does that make? In Italy, we still love him, we still listen to him, we still buy his records...." "I'm sorry, sir, we don't have his records because he's dead." "Well, how about Beniamino Gigli?" "Sorry, he's dead, too." "But what difference does that make? In Italy, we still love him, we still listen to him, we still buy his records...." "I'm sorry, sir." The poor diplomat mentioned a few more Italian tenors and was rebuffed each time. As he turned on his heel and stalked out of the store, muttering to himself, he noticed, out of the corner of his eye, a record by Mario Lanza. Meanwhile, Dad was attending to another customer. The diplomat turned around and called out, "Hey, you!" Dad excused himself and walked over.

"Yes?" "What's that?" "What's what?" "That record there!" "What about it?" "It's a record by Mario Lanza!" "So?" "He's dead!" "Oh, my God, when did he die?"

That was my father, the great leg-puller. And how about the great disciplinarian? Once, when we children were misbehaving and he had already told us several times to stop, he finally put his foot down. "That's it! Misbehave once more and you'll each get two smacks! Twice more and you'll get four smacks." And then the punch line: "And today we have a special—three for five!" At which point, Mom stormed in from the next room and announced, through gritted teeth: "Thank you very much for disciplining them!"

No, Itzik wasn't a clown. He was just an indefatigably quick wit who really did fill our lives with laughter.

Paul Glasser
August 2014

A Plentiful Bounty

Introduction by Josh Glazer

The stories that my Uncle Itzik wrote paint a vivid portrait of a family struggling through the Great Depression of the 1930s. Though laced with humor and told from the perspective of a child with a zest for life, the stories leave little doubt that the family's poverty was real. Money was scarce, food was limited, beds were shared, and luxuries consisted of scraping together a few pennies to go to the movies. The fact that my grandparents—with little skill, education, or money—managed to keep the family together is remarkable.

As I recount my uncle's and my father's stories, including some that my father told me but that are not written here (shivering in the night because his brother had wrapped himself around their one shared blanket), I am reminded of a perplexing riddle that has long intrigued me: How did the children of this family all become educated adults, firmly entrenched in middle-class life?

Social science is overflowing with reasons why this is a most unlikely outcome. The raw materials of academic success and social mobility are said to include homes whose walls are lined with books, parents who devote hours to helping with homework, private tutors, summer camps, trips abroad, music lessons, and the like. The recycling, resewing, and restoring (to borrow from my cousin Paul's introduction) that occupied my grandmother's days are not on the list. My grandfather's insightful commentaries on life—"He was born lousy, he's still lousy, and he'll always be lousy"—are the stuff of family legend, but I am not under the impression that he sat with his children to unpack the mechanics of multiplying fractions. The answer to the riddle apparently lies elsewhere.

* * * * *

Even if my father, Mickey Glazer, did not write about his career as a sociologist, a perceptive reader could well see that he viewed the world through a sociologist's lens. His keen eye for the human character, his detailed descriptions of events that took place decades earlier (his account of the Enright family details a dinner menu from 1959!), and his fascination with extraordinary individuals (of which there are plenty in the pages to come) go a long way toward describing the sociologist's toolbox—a toolbox that would serve him well for a career stretching over forty years. But if these stories reveal what my father would label "the sociological imagination," I can't help but think that they also provide some clues to the question of how he, his siblings, their friends, and countless other individuals who grew up in that particular place and time so remarkably transcended the poverty that defined their early lives.

This question, it turns out, has been raised by others. The sociologist James Coleman also wondered how it could be that an entire generation of New York Jews, many of whom grew up in the turmoil and despair of the Great Depression, went on to experience academic and economic success. For Coleman, the answer lay in the dense network of relationships so characteristic of the Brooklyn neighborhoods, the ones that are depicted so vividly in my father's and my uncle's stories. Coleman coined the phrase "social capital" as a way of suggesting that these relationships could be transformed into other types of social and economic resources. Might it be that characters such as Mrs. Youshak, Herman and Phil Teitelbaum, and cousin Mollie, described in my uncle's and my father's stories, were not merely a distraction from the daily grind of poverty, but the escape vehicle that would eventually take them to a better life?

Individuals, families, and neighborhoods being what they are, we can't really know the answer to this question. But I will allow my myself to imagine that the path leading upward from the vibrant but small world of Brooklyn was built not stone by stone, but person by person, story by story, by the likes of Mr. Enright, who modestly recounted to my twenty-five-year-old father how he rescued displaced children in the aftermath of World War II; by my father's roommate, Michel Wasserberger, who escaped from a German prisoner-of-war camp and then dedicated his life to working with troubled youth; by the gentle suggestion of Phil Teitelbaum to my twelve-year-old father and his friend Herman that they venture beyond their Brooklyn neighborhood into the larger world of Manhattan; and even by my grandfather, Ben Migdal, whose journey from Warsaw to a New York boardinghouse for homeless immigrants, and then to New Jersey, where he raised his family, is no less remarkable. In my mind, at least, the determination, grit, and imagination that propelled my father and his siblings to transcend the limitations of their childhood were born and nourished by these and countless other individuals like them.

But if this story about social mobility rests on more imagination than theory, there is one thing that does seem beyond doubt, and that is my father's lifelong fascination with individual fortitude and courage. Typing these names—Enright, Wasserberger, Teitelbaum, Migdal—the thread that runs through the various chapters of my father's life comes into view. Because while this may be his first foray into memoir, I can't help but see a tie between these stories and the academic work that defined his professional career. The characters depicted in his (and my mother's) academic books consist of individuals who discovered within themselves the wherewithal and courage to report nuclear waste, toxic orange juice, government fraud, and much more. My parents' work situated the actions of these remarkable people— "whistleblowers," they called them—in the context of community, family, and faith. But are they so different from the friends, roommates, and family members that are described in these short stories? Are the courage and conviction of Michel Wasserberger and Mr. Enright any less than that of Penny Newman, who led an environmental crusade in Riverside California, or of Lisa Crawford, who protested the unlawful dumping of nuclear waste? Is the perseverance and pluck of Ernest Fitzgerald, who exposed defense department waste, so different from that of my father's mother, Ida, who as a twelve-year-old Russian immigrant went to work in a factory, and then later kept her family intact through the poverty of the 1930s; or than that of my father's cousin, Mark Siegel, who resigned in protest from the Carter administration?

But, in the end, it doesn't really matter if comparing the nuclear activist Karen Silkwood to my grandmother Ida Glasser is a stretch, and it doesn't even matter if my musings about the family's escape from poverty are no more than that. Because what is truly compelling is my father's lifelong fascination with the capacity of individuals to overcome and transcend; to act in ways that in retrospect seem so admirable, but at the time required remarkable fortitude. If there is one thing that I take from these stories, it is that this fascination may have been polished at Rutgers, Princeton, and Smith College, but it was born in the second floor of a crowded and immaculately clean Brooklyn apartment. And in return for this, I offer the following entry into the official record: In the more than four decades of my father's professional career, he documented the extraordinary behaviors of courageous individuals. The stories of his own family, now finding their way into print, describe no less strength and determination.

Josh Glazer
August, 2014

Mickey and Josh

Yudis, Itz, and Mickey on Hegeman Avenue

Mickey on Hegeman Avenue

PART ONE

Welcome to East New York

443 HEGEMAN AVENUE

1

Itzik

When I was growing up, East New York and the neighborhood of Brownsville, in Brooklyn, New York was an exhilarating place inhabited mainly by the Ashkenazi Jews of Eastern Europe and the Sephardi Jews of the Middle East. Many of the residents were working-class poor, if they were lucky enough to be working, and for many families survival depended on trick mirrors, practiced fasting, and varying degrees of deprivation.

In the first nine years of my life, we moved six times because we couldn't afford to pay the exorbitant rents charged at the time. Who could afford thirty-five dollars a month when your father's business was bankrupt and he couldn't admit it?

At that time, moving was a simple procedure. You moved because some landlord offered three months of rent concession if you moved into his building. That, coupled with a newly painted apartment, was an attractive inducement. We would live in such an apartment for several months until, when my father's business went from bad to worse, we stopped paying the rent while the landlord threatened, cajoled, and finally instituted dispossession proceedings against us. How often I remember my father's defense for his actions as he explained to the landlord, "You can't get blood from a stone!"

And so, once again, we would move. I attended so many different schools during the first four years of my school life that the teachers called me "Hey, you."

"Hey, you, if you had fifty cents, and you spent ten cents, how much would you have left?"

"Fifty cents? First of all, I never had fifty cents. And if I had fifty cents, I wouldn't spend a dime."

"Okay, let's try again. If the movies cost ten cents, and you had four cents, how much more would you need to go to the movies?"

"Two milk deposit bottles," I answered.

That's how we thought and lived then. Until, at last, our luck suddenly changed—it got worse. In August 1934, when I was nine, and six weeks before my mother gave birth to her fourth child, Mickey, we moved to a tiny, four-room apartment. While it had only a coal stove in the kitchen for heating, we rented it because we hoped we could afford the twenty dollars a month rent.

It was 443 Hegeman Avenue, near Malta Street, in the southeastern part of East New York. While the apartment was tiny, it was situated in a neighborhood where there were no apartment buildings close by and had excellent shopping just one block north. To the south, just across Linden Boulevard, were empty lots stretching block after block, as far as the eye could see. I could run, play, race, shout, hide, and do whatever I liked, to my heart's content. So although the apartment was smaller, the neighborhood was poorer, and our home was heated by a stove in the kitchen, for me it was paradise. We ended up living on Hegeman Avenue for more than ten years. It was the first time I would make lasting friendships, and I would meet and fall in love with my first girlfriend. It was home.

Outside, the uncluttered streets offered my friends and me a kind of freedom I had never enjoyed before. We played and socialized in the streets and found ways to earn a few pennies to buy candy or ice cream. When the weather was pleasant, we would play punchball, stickball, or boxball with a three-cent rubber ball or, if we could afford the nickel, a Spalding rubber ball.

The apartments where we lived were always off-limits to my friends and me. That was an unwritten law. The bedrooms were always tiny. The living room was for company only, and the kitchen served as the center of our universe. It was for eating, doing homework, reading, and listening to the radio. Anyway, one reasoned, if your friends hung out long enough you might have to offer them a cookie, which was always in very short supply and needed to feed four hungry mouths. We refused to share our poverty.

I never visited a friend at his home. I would knock at the door and ask, "Is Philly home?"

"Yes, he'll be right out."

To be invited inside might cause problems. We had too much energy. What if we broke something? We were all too poor to take the chance. You waited outside or downstairs.

The basic necessities of life had to be approached pragmatically. We all agreed we needed food, clothing, and shelter. My mother had read it somewhere; it was as simple as that. My mother explained, "We don't need clothing. We'll manage with what we have. Between patching and hand-me-downs, we'll be all right." Buying clothes was out, with one important exception: I had to have sneakers for school and play. When my mother was able to save the ninety-nine cents, she would buy them for me. The sneakers I craved, U.S. Keds, cost a dollar and a quarter. While I longed for them, I knew we couldn't afford the extra pennies. As we left the store, my mother would admonish me each time, "Just be grateful I've bought you these. I don't want you to run and jump like a wild Indian. Make them last."

Food? Let's see, food. We ate only after the rent was paid. That concept was non-negotiable. We had to have a place to live!

As a poor but wise man once said, "How do I survive? I fast two days a week. If I didn't fast, I'd starve." We managed in the same way.

As the Great Depression continued, we accepted the hardships and tried to find ways to make life somewhat pleasant. In the evenings during the week, at suppertime and immediately after, we would sit in the kitchen and listen to the small radio that sat atop the icebox. My favorite programs were Jack Armstrong, the All-American Boy;

Tom Mix; and Bobby Benson. Radio offered us the opportunity to use our imaginations as we heard horses being ridden, the noises of a storm, dogfights between airplanes, or ships adrift at sea. The mystery stories, which we insisted on listening to, frightened and delighted us. Of course, at the end of each story, with all the adversity and tribulations, we were always happy when the good guys won.

Bobby Benson and Tom Mix offered wonderful adventure stories and free gifts if you were willing to buy the cereals they advertised and send in the box tops. I hated H-O Oats, I despised Ralston, but I needed the box tops. I would beg my mother to buy these cereals, insisting that they were healthy for me, but she refused.

"I won't buy it. You don't like them and you won't eat them."

"I'll eat it. I swear, please. I want to get the Tom Mix badge that makes me a straight-shooter."

I had little choice; I was forced to eat that sludge. I even remember searching through garbage cans in the hope of finding other empty boxes. Every empty box I found meant one less box of cereal I had to eat.

The only other alternative offered was when the announcer said, "Send in two box tops or a reasonable facsimile." I remember asking my sister Fay, the family genius, what a reasonable facsimile was. I received her usual response.

"Why don't you look it up in the dictionary, stupid?" That was her nickname for me. (When my mother asked her why, she answered, "Because I can't always remember his name.")

I listened to the adventures, ate the cereals, and was rewarded with a constant flow of badges, secret decoder rings, good luck charms, and the cowboy paraphernalia they offered. Each day, when I arrived home from school, I would make a mad dash for the mailbox, hoping to discover my latest prize or treasure.

My life was happiest whenever I managed to earn or get the few pennies necessary for the weekly trip to the local movie house, with an extra penny or two for candy. Two cents bought fourteen caramels. The challenge was in acquiring the few pennies.

How well I remember the few special occasions when my father seemed "rich" and offered me a king's ransom.

"If you could have any amount of money, how much would you ask for?" he asked.

"Any amount?" I replied.

"Any amount."

In that case, I would ask for twenty-seven cents."

He reached into his pocket, withdrew some change and handed me twenty-seven cents.

Then he asked, "Why twenty-seven cents?"

"Pop, do you know what I can buy with twenty-seven cents? Everything I want. I can afford to have lunch in the delicatessen with my friends. Two frankfurters with mustard and sauerkraut and a Pepsi-Cola. That's fifteen cents, and we don't have to tip the waiter. We eat at the counter. Then we go to the movies, that's ten cents, and I have enough left over for candy to last the whole show."

We had very little money, made every penny stretch, worked hard, bought things after much soul-searching, used everything well and carefully, savored every morsel, enjoyed every pleasure, cherished every gift, appreciated every generosity, and understood clearly our parents' struggle to survive.

2 RIDING INTO THE SUNSET

Mickey

My family lived on the second floor of a six-family house in Brooklyn, and on the third floor was my friend Herman Teitelbaum. We were friends from the time we were babies. We even drank bottles together on the landing between the second and third floors. His mother would put out a brown blanket, big enough for two toddlers to lie down with their milk. I never tired of rehearsing these childhood stories for my daughter Jessica, and she never tired of asking me questions about Herman and me as little kids. She wanted to know whether drinking bottles together was the only thing we did. I told her that Herman and I visited the shul around the corner on many Friday nights when we were about six or seven years old. Neither one of us was very interested in the service, but we relished the moment when there was the *Borei Pri Hagafen* blessing over the wine. The rabbi would give each of us a sip of the sweet wine, and we were so happy to be part of the special Shabbat ritual. (Don't worry, neither one of us ended up as an alcoholic, and our children relished the Manischevitz wine every Friday evening in much the same way.)

Herman and I loved all the cowboy heroes of our day. We thoroughly enjoyed listening to the radio programs that featured stars such as Gene Autry, Roy Rogers, Tom Mix, and, of course, the Lone Ranger and Tonto. From our affection for the masked man, it was natural for us to seek out our own make-believe horses so that we too could do good deeds on the open plains or the lawless towns of the West. We named our horses Silver, for the Lone Ranger's horse, and Scout, for the horse of the brave Tonto. The horses were immensely intelligent, and we were proud to ride them. Where did our horses come from? The two stone walls that flanked our stoop. We were so intent in riding them that over time we actually wore grooves into the thick cement. On command from us, the horses would whisk us away from the confines of 443 Hegeman Avenue. We bounded across Linden Boulevard and, through our imaginations, landed on the western plains. The good people there needed our help, and outlaws dreaded our arrival. To make the action even more fun, we finished each strenuous adventure with an ice-cream pop from the truck that came down our street.

Years passed, and the neighborhood and the building deteriorated. The steps of the stoop collapsed, and the house itself was taken down by the city. The only things that survived were the stone "horses" themselves. When I returned to the neighborhood as an adult, the indestructible "horses" remained as the only reminder that the Teitelbaums and the Glazers had actually lived in that building. Around the corner, on Malta Street, I saw a sheet of metal swinging in the wind with the words "Los Olvidados" painted on it. I understood as a sociologist that the people in this very poor area did indeed feel forgotten. But in my imagination, as long as Herman and I lived, as long as we maintained the bond of friendship, there was a chance, if only a chance, that the neighborhood would come back to life, that the horses would gallop once again through the shouts of delighted little children riding off into the sunset.

Herman was a frequent visitor to our apartment, and he often arrived just as we were having dinner. He would stand there, watching us eating, and somebody from my family would always ask if he would like to join us. My sister Fay was especially solicitous. She liked Herman and would make sure there was a bit of extra food to include him. Herman never forgot her kindness. Many, many years later, he sent her a beautiful bouquet of roses to help celebrate her ninetieth birthday. She had not seen him in more than a half century, and suddenly these delicate flowers arrived on her doorstep. She was absolutely shocked and delighted.

When we were about twelve years old, Herman's older brother Phil suggested that we would really enjoy taking a subway ride into Manhattan. What should we do there? Phil said that we might like the Museum of Modern Art. He said they showed an excellent film every Saturday afternoon and that we would really benefit from leaving our neighborhood and being a bit more adventurous. He also thought that we could even learn something about art while we were there. The subway ride was a nickel, and I don't think we had to pay any admission to the museum, so money was not an issue. I remember how much we loved the film, Mutiny on the Bounty, starring Clark Gable. I cannot vouch for how much we learned about art, but we did get a thrill out of playing the role of museum guide. We took turns interpreting the meaning of a painting and imagining the artist's intention. I can't remember any of the paintings we discussed, but I know that a couple of kids from Hegeman Avenue in Brooklyn were introduced to a whole new world of modern art. We must have seen Picassos, Matisses and van Goghs, all of which were new and strange to us.

When we told Phil how much we enjoyed Mutiny on the Bounty, he suggested that we read the trilogy on which the film was based. Those books, Mutiny on the Bounty, Men Against the Sea, and Pitcairn's Island became some of my favorites. During those years we went on to read Captain Horatio Hornblower, Captain Blood, and any other adventure stories we could find.

Much as we relished this foray into high culture, we remained kids who loved fun in all the places around us. When we were about sixteen, each of us had a part-time job that gave us a little bit of spending money. We had saved just enough to combine our resources and rent a locker in Coney Island. We treated ourselves to a summer of swimming and handball. We also liked the idea of looking at the pretty young girls in their stylish bathing suits. But of course we were much too shy to approach any of them—well, not always. Sometimes we managed to get out a weak "hello." Of course, we could not go to Coney Island without visiting Nathan's for their famous hotdogs and orange drinks. Standing on a long line waiting our turn, we became part of the mix of New Yorkers, old and young, Jew and Gentile, fat and slim, breathing in the delicious aromas that became stronger as we moved closer and closer to the counter. I was slight of build and easily pushed out of my turn, so I depended on having Herman, bigger, stockier, and stronger, standing next to me. I like to think that throughout our years together each of us felt more secure in the presence of the other.

Herman and I managed to keep seeing each other until well after the time that Herman moved away from Hegeman Avenue, but the distance made contact more difficult, and eventually we lost touch with each other. There was no Facebook, e-mail, or even cheap long-distance telephone service.

Over the years, I told Jessica that Herman was the only person I knew whose birthday fell on February 29 and that one day I would phone to wish him a happy birthday. I found out that he was working at the National Institutes of Health in Maryland. On February 29, 1980, about twenty years since I had last seen him, I phoned his office. The secretary asked whether she could inform Dr. Teitelbaum who was calling. I replied that I was an old friend and would rather tell him myself. When Herman answered the phone, I said, "Happy Birthday, Herman, from 443 Hegeman Avenue." Of course, Herman immediately recognized my voice, and the bonds of friendship were renewed. Since then, we always speak on our birthdays and try to connect at other times. Our conversations these days are less about the old neighborhood and more about our children and grandchildren. Although I have these kinds of discussions with many people, there is something special about having Herman back in my life. In this world of constant change and so many severed ties, I cherish the continuity that comes from a lifetime of friendship.

Fay starting Brooklyn College at age 15

Siegel family at Beverly and Paul's wedding in 1947
— Jerry is the cool teenager sitting on the left.

PART TWO

Family Forever

MY SISTER, THE MONSTER   3

Itzik

I'm firmly convinced that MGM Studios did not originate the idea of introducing each movie with a roaring lion. They stole it from my sister Fay, who had started doing it some years earlier whenever she was angry. When you asked her a question while she was engrossed in reading or disturbed her in any way when she didn't want to be disturbed, she would roar ominously through clenched teeth, demanding, "What is it? Leave me alone! Stop talking to me! Do it yourself! Get away! When are you going to learn to do things on your own?"

These were all rhetorical questions since, at the first roar, you were already heading for the hills. And if there were no hills to head for, you were anxious to rush out and build some.

She was a monster, a terror, who was at once unreasonable, arbitrary, overbearing, dictatorial, intimidating, or, as I said several hundred times as we were growing up, "just a rotten person."

She frightened everyone indiscriminately. The family bully, Cousin Phil, abused everybody both verbally and physically, but he was smart enough to keep his distance from Fay. He knew that in any battle with her, he was doomed to lose. She cut you to pieces with words. They said that her bark was worse than her bite. The truth was that they were both pretty scary.

Now what made Fay so formidable? She was tall for her age, with an athletic-looking body on a large frame. Her long, wavy blond hair and her seemingly Scandinavian good looks made her the neighborhood beauty. She walked with an air of confidence that seemed to say, "Keep your distance." To add to this, she was highly intelligent and a voracious reader, with a great thirst for knowledge. By the time she entered junior high school, she had been skipped four times. As her fame spread throughout our extended family, she received strange compliments, such as, "If she's as smart as they claim, who does she take after?"

Fay, it seemed, knew everything. Whatever you needed to know, it was "ask Fay." But while it was obvious that she was gifted in many ways, as far as I was concerned, she was an uncooperative horror.

She spent every spare minute reading at the kitchen table—the only available place in the small apartment. The crowded living room was filled with overstuffed pieces and was off-limits to us. Fay couldn't and wouldn't be interrupted for any reason. If you wanted to ask her a question, her demeanor seemed to indicate "Caution! Proceed at your own risk."

If that scenario didn't frighten you, she had another habit that made us want to climb walls. She would go into the bathroom to read and refuse to come out when anyone else needed to use it. Whatever time it was, she would roar, "I just got in here and I'll come out when I'm good and ready." Eventually, if you begged her and bothered her long enough, making it impossible for her to continue reading, she would reluctantly come out from her "private library." Since she was annoyed with you for making her leave her domain, she usually whacked you on the head as she passed by.

The one, small radio we had, which sat atop the icebox, was supposed to be shared by everybody in the house. That was the rule. However, whenever Fay came home from school or the library, she would walk into the house and, without asking, flip the radio dial from my stories or a ball game or whatever I was listening to, announcing, "You've had your turn with the radio. Now it's my turn." She would turn the radio dial to WQXR and her stupid classical music. When I complained bitterly about listening to that horrible noise, she had the same stock answer: "Stupid, without this terrible noise, all your boring stories would be nothing. It's Rossini, Weber, Beethoven, Mendelssohn, and Wagner that add the excitement." I knew she was wrong. After all, I reasoned, if any of them were as good as she said, they'd be playing for the New York Yankees.

Fay had an aura about her that intimidated people. I remember watching her occasionally as she walked past the boys who hung out at the local candy store. They stood outside in small groups and, as girls strolled by, they whistled and made offensive remarks. When Fay walked by, they looked and they thought their thoughts, but they said nothing. They knew that she might respond with a blistering verbal attack that would embarrass them in front of their friends—a prospect they didn't crave.

Surprisingly, while Fay and I often fought about the arrogant manner in which she attempted to impose her tastes upon me, I frequently found myself bragging to my friends about this "miserable person" who was so smart that she knew everything. She read The Sunday New York Times while the rest of us read the Daily News, she listened to classical music while the rest of us listened to popular music, and she was always the youngest and brightest girl in her class.

In her last year of high school, there was a family crisis. Even though she was still my nemesis because she continually pushed me around, I was able to commiserate with her. She had a dilemma and she couldn't be certain of the outcome. She was fifteen years old at the time, and when she mentioned to her favorite teacher that she might not be permitted to continue her education after high school, the principal was notified. He sent my father a letter strongly suggesting, if at all financially possible, that a student of her caliber be encouraged to attend college.

My father was adamantly opposed to the idea. We were poor. We needed the few dollars she would earn each week if she went to work instead. He reasoned "wisely" that girls didn't have to go to college. After all, he believed their future was more or less predetermined. They would finish high school, work for a short period, and get married. Why waste the time, energy, and money on something as foolish as higher education?

Fay appealed to our mother: "Ma, I have to. I want to go to college very much. Please help me." My mother, who had never learned to read and write because of her mother's attitude toward daughters, thought about her own daughter's anguish and replied to Fay, "If I help you go to college, do you understand I won't be able to give you any spending money, buy you clothes, or help you in any way?"

My sister said," It doesn't matter, Ma. I want to go."

My mother had great difficulty discussing this issue with my father. While she feared his anger, she insisted that the decision belonged to my sister, and that as long as Fay understood that no monetary help would be forthcoming, she could go to college. The year was 1937, and my mother said that we would find a way to struggle on without the few dollars my sister might earn.

Fay attended college with a wardrobe consisting of three blouses and two skirts. She had to wash, clean, and press her clothes almost daily. She used no makeup and never went to a beauty parlor. She even managed to contribute part of her fifteen-dollar-a-month salary, which she earned from working in the Brooklyn College library, to help support the family.

She was the oldest grandchild in the family and the first person to attend college. While she struggled and worked her way through four years of school, she thrived—loving every minute of it—and she graduated, as usual, with honors.

During her senior year of college, she met Terry. Terry was her intellectual equal but he was a ninety-seven-pound weakling, and when I noticed the relationship becoming serious, I felt honor bound, man to man, to warn him of his impending danger. He was doomed to become enmeshed in a trap like mine, in which he would be forced to listen to classical music, follow unacceptable guidelines of behavior, and never know for certain when he would be allowed to use the bathroom. And why? All because she was bigger and stronger than he was. Realizing that time was running out, I took him aside one day and said, "Terry, as much as I want to get rid of my sister, I feel compelled to tell you what she's really like." I proceeded to tell him what life with Fay had been like. He thanked me and said he would take it under advisement. Some months later, without discussing it with me, Terry gave Fay a wrist watch as an engagement present. I knew the poor fool had been snared.

When he was transferred to New York from his job in Washington, D.C., they decided it was time to marry. Two months later, during the early summer of 1942, and with only their immediate families present, they were married in a simple ceremony in a small Jewish chapel in Brooklyn.

Because of Terry's influence, it seemed to me that Fay became less and less of a monster. I almost thought I was getting to like her. Her moving out meant several wonderful things. I was now the owner of an extra dresser drawer, I was allowed extended bathroom privileges, and I had more radio time and fewer clouts on the head.

I was grudgingly forced to admit two things to myself. First, I discovered that as Fay was getting older, I seemed to be getting smarter. Somewhere along the way, I had learned to appreciate classical music, foreign films, The Sunday New York Times, various ethnic restaurants in the city, Broadway plays, and many of the museums and other cultural activities that made living in New York exciting and special. Could I admit it? That I owed it all to the "monster" on the first floor at 443 Hegeman Avenue, Fay? Second, I realized that my father had indeed been "right" all along. Sending a girl to college was indeed a waste—as far as he was concerned. Shortly after she graduated, she became engaged, married, and moved out of the house. The return on his investment was indeed meager, just as my father had foreseen, foresworn, and predicted.

"Nu, so what have I been saying all along?" he was overheard saying to his friends. "The minute daughters start bringing a little money into the house, they run off, get married, and move away." Years later, when she began teaching, my father was so impressed. "Can you imagine," he told his friends, "she makes a good salary and gets benefits too. Who would have known that?"

Finding Jerry   4

Mickey

The schoolyard at P.S. 233 was busy one bright, sunny Sunday morning in May of 1948. My cousin, Jerry Siegel, played a rough game of touch football with his high school buddies. It was much too physical a game for my slight, thirteen-year-old body. But there were many other choices. Some of my friends played stickball against the wall where my friend, Mel, was a champ. In another part of the schoolyard, six boys, including me, were playing three-on-three basketball, which was much more to my liking. This was especially so when I scored an impressive driving layup, and the guy covering me was unexpectedly complimentary. I acted as if it was an everyday occurrence, but Burt insisted that it was worth a pat on the back. (I couldn't imagine that this boy, one I barely knew, would later become my best friend and the best man at my wedding.) If the basketball game was too fast, you could join a pickup game of slow-as-molasses softball. Even if you didn't enjoy the game, you could get a head start on your summer suntan as you waited endlessly for your turn at bat.

P.S. 233 was perfectly located. It was only a short walk from the corner apartment house where Jerry's parents, my cousins Chana and Dave Siegel, lived on the first floor. Chana was my father's favorite niece. She was the child of his oldest sister and only a few years younger than he. At the time, my family lived on Hopkinson Avenue, only a few blocks away—easy walking distance. I was a frequent visitor to their apartment with my father. On this particular Sunday, he sat down to share a bagel and talk with Chana and Dave, and I headed on to the schoolyard. Chana alerted me that her daughter and son-in-law, Beverly and Paul Radow, would be visiting. Most likely, Chana told me, they would stop by the schoolyard to see Jerry and me. Knowing Paul, I was sure he could be enticed to shoot a few baskets with me and my friends. But basketball was only part of the reason for my excitement. I was always so happy to be in Paul's company. Not only was he a really good guy, happy to show me a few pointers in my basketball game, but he was also tall and good-looking. To know that I could bring this six-foot-plus guy to the game enhanced my status with my friends by several inches. (I should add that I recently had dinner with Paul and Beverly. They are still a strikingly handsome couple. Beverly and I picked up our conversation as if there had not been decades of separation, and Paul continued to radiate that special charm that so captivated me sixty-five years ago.)

But Sunday in my family was not only for schoolyard games. The day always included the special ritual of visiting relatives. My father and I may have started the day at Chana and Dave's, but the main focus of the afternoon was the weekly visit to my mother's family. Most often, we traveled to Flushing, Queens, where two of my mother's brothers and one of her sisters lived. Initially, my father had few complaints about the long hours of visiting. There were frequent discussions about the best place to live in New York—Brooklyn versus Queens—and arguments with his brothers-in-law about the cemetery purchase for the newly formed Peretz family circle. Meanwhile, the women talked among themselves and prepared the evening meal.

Despite my father's pleasure in these Sunday outings, over time he began to resent what he saw as the increasing dominance of my mother's family in our lives. He began to complain that his family was not getting equal weight. I think this began when Itz, Estelle, Fay, and Terry formed a circle of friends with several of our first cousins on my mother's side. These people became more than just cousins in name; a group of them became lifelong friends. These relationships were built on a strange convergence of a penchant for radical politics and an affinity for the more elite culture of museums, theater, and concerts. But most salient was a concern with fashion and furnishings. My cousin Molly became the arbiter of good clothes and well-decorated apartments. Everyone went shopping with Molly so that they could be sure to meet the test of good taste. Even at age seventeen, when I was living in a working-class section of Brooklyn, taken with left-wing ideas and concern for the poor, I went with my earnings as a delivery boy to shop for a beautiful cashmere sweater and expensive argyle socks with Molly. The next year I was very proud of a sport jacket that I purchased at the upscale men's shop, Rogers Peet, at Molly's urging of course. Initially, when I saw the jacket I thought that it was much too expensive, at $52. "Why do you take me to see such beautiful clothes that I can't afford?" But in the end Molly helped me figure out that there was a way, and I wore that jacket for years to come.

It's not that members of my father's family were slackers. Chana and Dave's children all went on to professional lives. Jerry became a doctor. Their son-in-law Paul was an engineer, and their youngest son, Mark, earned a Ph.D. and went on to a distinguished career in politics.

But as we grew older, my family saw them less and eventually lost touch completely when the older generation was no longer around to bring the family together. There was some sadness for me in losing touch with these cousins. I treasured plenty of good memories of our times with that part of my extended family. I can still remember the day in 1947, during a historic snowstorm, when Jerry and I banded together to go house-to-house soliciting business for our snow-shoveling service. We were rewarded by a plentiful bounty of jobs and, for us, a financial windfall. Despite my junior status, I'm pretty sure we split the take evenly. Rarely had I been involved in such a profitable venture, and I went home proud to be flush with cash.

I also remember Jerry's bar mitzvah very clearly. The part that made the biggest impression on me was what happened when he finished his haftorah and the prayers that follow it. As was the tradition, kids in the congregation threw an avalanche of candy at him from every direction. In the split second before the candy landed on him, Jerry ducked down beneath the bima for protection. I admired his quick decision and good reflexes. I was particularly impressed that he refused to be a victim, even in the spirit of candy and good fun. I thought my cousin Jerry really was savvy and determined then and there to do the same thing at my bar mitzvah.

Some years later, Jerry left the city and so did I. But I continued to see Chana and Dave on visits to my parents and on special occasions. Chana was so happy when Penina and I told her that Penina was pregnant, and she came to Northampton on the occasion of Josh's bris. We have a memorable photo of her coming into the house with my mother, both laden with shopping bags filled with bread, cake, lox, and whitefish from Brooklyn. After all, where else could you find the food to celebrate the birth of our first child?

Even after most of the contacts with my father's family ended, there were a few exceptions. For a number of years I kept in touch with my cousin Mark. He had been a White House aide to President Carter; he resigned in protest when he was not informed of a secret sale of military aircraft to Saudi Arabia. Mark was liaison between the White House and the Jewish community and had repeated to the leaders of the major Jewish organizations what he had been told—that there had not been any such sale. Mark's resignation made him a hero in the Jewish community but persona non grata in White House circles. When Penina and I were writing our book on whistleblowers in the 1980s, I had a long discussion with Mark about the centrality of loyalty above principle for those who want to rise in Washington politics. After that I kept in touch with Mark and Judy for a number of years. We went to their son's bar mitzvah with my parents, who made their only trip to Washington, D.C. for the occasion. But, like many families with busy schedules and living far apart, through distraction and neglect, we all allowed the relationship to fall away.

Then, in 2008, I received an unexpected phone call from Penina's sister Ayala. She generally speaks to Penina four or five times a week, so her call did not seem unusual until she said, "Put Mickey on the phone. I have something amazing to tell him." She then went on to recount the story of her friend Rita, who had been widowed and then remarried. Rita and her husband had been visiting some friends in the Berkshires. Those friends shared a story about a visit to the Yiddish Book Center in Amherst, Massachusetts. In the course of the conversation, the friends mentioned that Ayala's sister, Penina, was on the board of directors of the book center. "Penina?" Rita's husband asked. "I know a Penina. Is her husband Mickey Glazer? If so, he's my cousin." Ayala had met Jerry a number of times but had no idea that he was related to me. And so, a phone call later, much to my delight, Jerry and I found each other. My first reaction was a combination of surprise and pleasure. So many years had passed since I'd had any news of him. By this time, Jerry had retired and lived much of the year in Florida, so we arranged to meet there on our next visit to my daughter Jessica. Jerry and Rita also invited Beverly and Paul, as well as his uncle Irv. It was our first occasion to catch up on various family members and remember old times.

Why did I care so much about reconnecting? Jerry told me it mattered to him because it made him feel younger. For me, it was even more emotional. On one level, we were unfamiliar with each other's adult lives, in some ways strangers gathering a quick summary of half a century. Yet, at the same time, I could close my eyes and with a little imagination see my father bursting through the door of Chana and Dave's apartment on a Sunday morning, ebulliently expressing his pleasure at seeing Jerry and me together.

The next year we came down to Florida to prepare for a particularly happy occasion. Jessica and Doug were having their first baby, and we knew it would be a boy. Penina and I were in charge of making arrangements for the bris. We called Jerry to see whether he could suggest the name of a moel. He immediately recommended a pediatrician/moel who had performed the circumcision for his own grandson. The doctor, an Orthodox Jew, was particularly sensitive to issues surrounding circumcision, rejecting some traditional views that eight-day-old children did not experience pain.

We were very pleased that Rita and Jerry shared this simcha with us. Jerry served as the sandek, the person who holds the baby during the circumcision. Traditionally this is a position of honor in the ceremony. Given his medical background, Jerry also assisted in the procedure, making things easier for the nervous parents and grandparents. It was special for us because it represented continuity of the generations. Just as we had valued his mother's presence at Josh's bris, for me, Jerry's participation in Justin's meant that my father and his family were there in spirit. Pa would have been thrilled at the birth of his fifteenth great-grandchild. He certainly would have declared his famous blessing to all of us: "Your life should be as sweet as you make mine."

Chocolate Pudding   5

Itzik

"You're sitting with one foot out the door again" was my mother's constant complaint about me at meals. "How many times do I have to tell you to finish eating and sit for a minute before you go out to play?"

I'm a skinny eight-year-old kid and we're living in a small apartment in Brownsville, Brooklyn. It's summertime, and the wonderful sounds of children playing beckon to me through our open third-floor windows.

"Finish every last bite. Remember, all the strength of the food is in the last piece."

I search my plate carefully, hoping to find the last piece. If I can eat that first, I won't have to finish everything. "Which is the last piece?" I ask my mother.

"How should I know?" she replies.

Then I say, "If you knew, would you tell me?"

"Yes," she assures me.

Then I say, "Help me. Give me a hint. What do you think?"

At this point, my mother is exasperated and ends the discussion in her usual manner: "Children are starving in Europe. It's a sin to waste food. Eat it all and stop annoying me."

And so it went. On those occasions when I finished eating a meal without a fuss, I remember well how satisfying it was to realize that

I had single-handedly saved children in Europe from starving, although I was never certain how that actually worked.

At that time, we were also concerned with dieting, but diets were to help you gain weight, not lose it. Ads admonished us to eat Wonder Bread: "Helps build strong bodies twelve ways."

My two older sisters stood by, listening to my recurring conversation with my mother with obvious displeasure. Why does he always have to get special treatment? they asked. They were more aware than I of how scarce money was, and they resented my mother's attempt to cater to my strange eating preferences. "I want the white meat, not the dark meat. Take off the skin. Okay, I'll eat the fish but only the 'clean' parts, and make sure there are no bones." Eggs had to be prepared in a certain way, and I would never eat or even taste food that didn't pass my visual inspection. "I don't want eggplant. I don't like the way it looks."

"Taste it. You might like it."

"No, I won't eat it. I won't like it." So even though everyone else loved it, my mother made her favorite eggplant dish infrequently. My sisters, who always felt it necessary to intrude upon my private conversations, shouted, "He doesn't need a mother ... he needs a French chef!"

But after all, I was the skinny one. More important, I was the only son after two unsuccessful attempts, according to my father. And he carefully taught me that "a man is a man." Men were the bosses. Women were meant to do their bidding and cater to their wishes.

"When you finish your dessert, you can go down to play," my mother said. I was anxious to leave, as always, but dessert was the best part of the meal.

Saying this, my mother placed before me the dessert that she had prepared especially for me: My-T-Fine chocolate pudding, a treat fit for a king, almost as good as ice cream.

As I looked down at the dish she had removed from the icebox and placed before me, I was startled.

"What's this?" I asked.

"Chocolate pudding. What do you think?"

"I mean, what's the white stuff all over it?" I demanded. "What did you do to it?"

"It's a little sweet cream."

It seems my mother's overriding ambition in life was to introduce me as follows. "I want you to meet my fat son, Irving. He used to be skinny, but with God's help I made him fat." I even remember her showing me a storybook when I was younger. She pointed to a picture of Humpty Dumpty, sighed, and said, "I'll bet he's a very good eater."

Sweet cream made you fat. But we couldn't afford sweet cream. So where did we get the sweet cream? At that time, they hadn't begun to homogenize milk. The cream in the milk always floated to the top. My mother had taken the bottle and carefully poured out some of the cream for me.

"I don't want it with sweet cream. I don't like it!" I shouted.

This was not the first such incident. A friendly neighbor who had finished high school and, therefore, knew everything had convinced my mother that in order to be healthy, I should drink a teaspoonful of cod liver oil every day. She bought the cod liver oil and had me try a spoonful. The taste was so awful that I swore to myself that no matter what, I would never be forced to eat anything again. The next morning, I was adamant. I refused to take the oil, saying, "You'll have to kill me first."

With the chocolate pudding, my mother said, "What do you mean, you don't like it? Taste it. It's delicious."

"I don't want it with sweet cream. It's spoiled. I'm not going to eat it."

My sisters watched silently from the sidelines. Another storm was brewing. The little *mamzer* was getting his way again after our mother had intentionally skimmed some of the sweet cream from the top of the milk, their milk, for him. All because I was skinny and the boy of the family—not necessarily in that order. I could read their thoughts, and that made me more intransigent. I had no intention of losing this battle.

"Eat it."

"No."

"Taste it."

"No. If you kill me, I won't taste it."

"It's not cod liver oil," she cried. "At least taste it."

"I don't like it. I don't want it. I just want plain chocolate pudding."

"All right," she said with resignation. "I'll take off the sweet cream."

"No. It's too late. It's spoiled."

"What do you mean, spoiled?"

"The cream has already touched the chocolate pudding."

The last remark I made enraged my sisters. "Make him try it!" they shouted. "Force him!"

My mother was wiser. She knew what an *akshn*, a mule, I was. Hitting wouldn't work. She had a better plan. She said, "If you don't eat it, or at least try it, you can't go down to play. Go to your bedroom, get undressed, and get ready for bed."

Painfully, but stubbornly, I refused to surrender, "I don't care. I won't go down. I won't eat it with sweet cream. I hate it with sweet cream."

So I went to my room. My mother put the chocolate pudding back in the icebox and a calm settled once more on the house.

In my room, I sat near the open window. Not only was the street filled with my friends and other children playing, but across from our windows there was a park and playground a square block long with swings, sliding ponds, a kiddie pool, and baseball fields, completely full.

As I looked out on this scene, a Bruegel painting brought to life, I longed to be part of it. But how? How could I reach a compromise without compromising? From the kitchen, I could hear the voices of my sisters complaining to my mother about the special attention I always received. Why was I special? They knew the answer and resented me for it.

"He's a boy."

"So what?!"

I could hear the screams of joy as delighted children took advantage of the extra summer daylight. The noises from the street were becoming more and more painful. I had to go down to play. But how? Suddenly, I remembered my mother's exact words. I didn't have to eat it. I only had to taste it. One taste and then I was free to leave. It's so easy to outfox mothers, I thought.

I yelled into the kitchen. "Ma, can I talk to you? Can I come out?" I waited for her answer.

And then she said, "Yes. Come."

I walked into the kitchen cautiously, paused, and then my eight-year-old mind sprang the trap on her. "I don't have to eat the chocolate pudding with the sweet cream? I only have to taste it and then I can go down to play?"

"Yes, just taste it. And if you don't like it, you don't have to finish eating it."

God, I thought, she's so gullible. I almost felt sorry for her. But then, mothers are supposed to be good, kind people ... softies.

"Okay, I'll try it," I said.

She went to the icebox, removed the dish with the chocolate pudding, got a spoon from the drawer, and placed this strange-looking concoction in front of me. I dipped the spoon into the dish and, with an obvious show of great displeasure, brought it slowly to my mouth. In one motion I consumed the spoonful before I could change my mind.

Suddenly, bells went off: "Idiot, this stuff is delicious," a voice in my mind said. "You never had it so good. Quickly, finish it before she changes her mind."

"So?" said my mother waiting for my response. "How is it?"

For a moment, I was too busy eating to answer her. When I had finished, I sheepishly looked up at her and before thinking about what I should say, I blurted out, "It's absolutely delicious. Make it this way all the time."

My mother was angry that I had made such a fuss before trying it, but my sisters were apoplectic. I believe that only the law of the land prevented them from killing me. Of course, I could tell that they were hatching new plans for future tortures of their little brother.

I ran out of the apartment, realizing that my mother's anger might translate at any moment into her breaking her promise about my going downstairs. The battle had been won, but the war wasn't over. I knew that the lecture to follow when I returned would be worth the hour of pleasure with my friends on that summer evening.

Josh and Jess traveling together

Itz as a teenager

PART THREE

Workers & Entreprenuers

An Arresting Experience   6

Itzik

One fateful morning, I awoke to find my father already dressed, nearly finished with his breakfast, and about to leave for work, so I knew that everything was all right. Meanwhile, my mother was scanning the morning paper, and when she came to page eight, she let out a gasp: "Oh, my God! Look at this—it's terrible. Now the whole world will know!" I took a look and was delighted and proud to see my father's picture in a major newspaper. The picture showed him in police custody, and the accompanying story clearly outlined the "crime" he had committed. I could hardly wait to show the picture to all my friends. After all, no one in our family had ever appeared in a newspaper before.

It was 1932 and I was seven years old. Business was slightly worse than terrible. Once the Depression came, men and women had to do whatever was necessary just to feed their families. My father owned a small printing shop on Sutter Avenue in Brooklyn and was desperate for work

To hear my father tell it, when two well-dressed young men entered his printing shop and identified themselves as New York University students authorized to have tickets printed for a forthcoming N.Y.U. dance, he was only too happy to oblige. The two men provided him the copy, left the required deposit, and were told when they could return to pick up the finished job. It is possible that my father neglected to ask questions for fear that he would have to refuse the order, but I don't know.

Several days later, they returned as instructed, checked the information on the ticket, were satisfied, paid the balance due, and left. The transaction completed, my father gave the matter no further thought. Imagine his surprise the following week when an official-looking city employee—as my father said, you could spot them a mile away—entered his store, identified himself as a police detective, produced a sample of the dance ticket, showed it to my father, and asked simply, "Do you recognize this ticket and did you print it?"

My father's answer was a straightforward "yes," whereupon the detective informed him that he was under arrest on a charge of printing counterfeit tickets. My father was shocked. He protested, recounted the incident from beginning to end, and explained how he had come to take the order. Claiming that the two college boys had shown him proper identification that proved that they were students at N.Y.U., he never thought to question their authorization to have the tickets printed.

It turned out that the enterprising young men were trying to defray some of the costs of their education by having additional tickets printed, which they hoped to sell without being discovered. As luck would have it, the organizers of the dance became suspicious when the dance was an unforeseen success—it was over-attended by several hundred. Thus when the two entrepreneurs were arrested, they were only too eager to share the blame with my father. They gave the police his bill, which showed where the tickets had been printed.

My father was taken to the local precinct, where he was fingerprinted and booked. The photo of this "notorious counterfeiter" was taken by a newspaper photographer and appeared in the next morning's edition.

My father was then brought before a judge. He offered his explanation of the strange chain of events, was released on bail, and returned home. At his trial, with a lawyer, he was able to convince the judge that he had indeed been duped by two unscrupulous college boys. He was acquitted with the admonition that ignorance of the law is no excuse. He was told that it was his responsibility to check for proper credentials before printing anything that could be redeemed for cash.

So ended my father's day in court and his life of crime, and with it my ability to brag to my friends about my famous father. If only my grandfather, the bootlegger, had been caught selling his bathtub gin—I could have started a scrapbook.

The Soda Kid

Itzik

Growing up in Brooklyn during the 1930s, I remember how I felt during the summer when the weather was very hot for several days in a row: miserable and thoroughly delighted.

It may seem like a contradiction, but while I certainly disliked the hot, humid weather, it enabled me to embark on an entrepreneurial adventure where I would learn buying, selling, merchandising, marketing, and public relations skills. Of course, at the time when I was thirteen years old, I didn't view it in such a profound way. My goal was a more practical one. If I were successful, I would have a job in which I was my own boss, I would have fun, and in just a few short hours I would return home having earned fifty cents.

In order to accomplish this memorable feat, earning fifty cents, I would become a soda kid for a day.

During the summer of 1938, when the weatherman on the radio predicted a "scorcher," I would go down into the basement of my house and *shlep* up the makeshift wagon that my friends had helped me build from four old carriage wheels, a two-by-four for a shaft, an old wooden orange crate, and a piece of wood as a steering column at the front end, with a rope attached to it. Into the crate I would stick a large, metal container and off I would go to the local soda distributor.

Once there, I would pick my way through the different brands, which the owner had laid out on the floor for easy access. I made my careful selection of twenty-four bottles of assorted flavors that I believed would sell easily. The selection process was critical because the profit, the end result of my day's labor, was based on selling all my wares.

Let's see. What did the thirsty drinking public demand? First, twelve-ounce bottles. After all, they were spending a nickel at a time when less-known brands sold for three cents. Coca-Cola at the time came in six-ounce bottles and was not considered a best buy when, for the same price, you could buy a twelve-ounce Pepsi-Cola. Twelve Pepsis and twelve bottles of assorted flavors—orange, cherry, and cream sodas, and ginger ale. You made the selection while keeping in mind that if you didn't have a customer's first choice, what you did have remaining should satisfy his second choice.

Having completed the selection, I then paid for the soda, sixty-five cents for a case of twenty-four bottles plus fifty cents deposit to be redeemed on returning the empties, and loaded it into the large, metal container. The entire transaction hinged on my ability to obtain the necessary funds for my venture-capital enterprise. Fortunately, I had found a banker with a heart, one who would lend me the money for a day at 0 percent interest—my mother, if, indeed, she had the enormous sum of $1.20 at all.

Before going on my way, I made sure I had my most essential tool, the bottle-opener. As a matter of fact, I took two: one hung from a long string nailed to the side of the wagon; the second was safely hidden in my pocket in case of an unforeseen emergency, such as someone stealing the first one.

My next stop was the nearby ice dock, where Sam, the ice man and neighborhood drunk, was prevailed upon to give me a five-cent piece of ice, which, I hoped, would be large enough to last for several hours while making and keeping the soda ice cold. Sam always treated me well because I never made fun of him the way the other kids did when he staggered about after a binge. After cutting the chunk of ice, Sam would also chop the ice into pieces small enough to slide in and among the soda bottles. The tin was then covered with an old potato sack that helped keep the cold in and the ice from melting too quickly.

Always somewhat apprehensive about letting me wander so far from home, my mother nevertheless wished me luck and helped me on my way by preparing my lunch, usually a buttered roll, an apple or banana, and a bottle of water. Making fifty cents was the important goal and I refused to drink any of my profits. Of course, I never drank the water in front of a potential customer. All this painstaking preparation was done early and took about an hour. Everything was finished so that I would reach my first important stop, a local schoolyard or park, at about eleven o'clock in the morning and still be on time to reach the road builders at about noon, when they broke for lunch.

At the local schoolyard, I would time my "Hey, get your ice-cold soda here!" between innings, when one team was about to come up to bat. At that point, my shouts would bring several of the players over and my first sales for the day were made. I stayed and waited for the empty bottles to be returned and then immediately left in time to reach my second stop, the most important one of the day.

I would venture forth from East New York and pull and push my heavy wagon loaded with soda and ice into Canarsie, a sparsely populated area about two miles from my house. Here, in the hot, unrelenting sun with no shade anywhere, the road crews, made up mostly of Italian immigrants, were digging up earth and laying down asphalt as they built Flatlands Avenue into a new four-lane road running east to west. To paraphrase General Custer, it was here that I had decided to make my last stand. As I crossed Linden Boulevard with some trepidation and ventured south into that strange no-man's land, I remembered that "Go to Canarsie" was a cry uttered when friends wanted you exiled to the end of the world: Canarsie, the land of marshes, beyond which lay the waters leading to the ocean.

When the lunch whistle blew, I would strategically locate myself at the spot where the crew would gather to sit. The workmen all seemed to dress in a similar fashion: in heavy work shoes and work pants, with only an undershirt on top, a bandanna around their neck to catch their sweat, and a cap to protect them from the sun. As they opened their lunch pails filled with overstuffed hero sandwiches and fruit, I would move quickly among them, answering questions about my assortment and selling as many sodas as possible in the few minutes that it took them to settle down for lunch. My "Hey, get your ice-cold soda here!" had to be an honest advertisement. A warm soda might create a threat, a reproach, even an international incident or, worst of all, a demand for the return of the nickel. It was truly the height of adventure, since the entire endeavor was a race against time. All the sodas had to be sold while they were still cold.

After the workers had finished lunch and returned the empty bottles, it was time to move on to the next site. Before doing this, I rearranged the remaining bottles and took inventory so I would know what I still had to sell. I also rearranged the remaining ice so that it would last as long as possible.

The number of bottles left would determine where I went next. I would always choose a place where I was the only vendor and where there were enough people to sell the few remaining sodas of a now limited assortment. Of course, if the weather was hot enough and the road crew large enough, I might possibly sell the entire case during the lunch break. Or, if I had very few sodas left, the men on the road gang might ask me to stay and wait another hour for their next break. When this happened and I was lucky, even when I was down to one or two bottles, they would be grabbed immediately.

At this point I would thank the men, collect the empty bottles, and start for home. On the way I would find some shady spot and eat my lunch, beaming at the fact that in only a few short hours I had made the fantastic sum of fifty cents. Not impressed? Fifty cents, when movies cost a dime, candy a penny, and a hot dog or soda only five cents each. For the next two weeks, I was wealthy beyond my wildest dreams.

I was very tired and hot from the long hours in the blazing sun, I marched the two miles back to the soda distributor to turn in my empty bottles with a wonderful feeling of pride and joy.

It was never too hot, nor was I too tired when I strode back into the house and told my mother what I had accomplished. I would count out the nickels, dimes, and quarters and hand her the money, telling her to use whatever part she needed to buy food or other necessities. I hoped, of course, that she would be able to return some part of it to me for a weekly allowance to spend on all the wonderful junk food and entertainment I could think of.

Weather permitting, that is, when it was very hot, I would sell sodas from my homemade wagon several times during the summer vacation, with varying degrees of success. The joy of this adventure came from the challenge and the sense of accomplishment. I had gone out into the world and conquered it, at least for one day; I had earned fifty cents. And although my world was usually the immediate neighborhood near our apartment, I had learned and succeeded in the bigger world beyond, at an enterprise of my choosing.

I earned fifty cents at a time when grown-ups, working long hours, five days a week, earned only five or six dollars for their efforts ... a dollar a day if they were lucky enough to find a job. My father left for his printing shop each morning at seven thirty and worked until ten at night six days a week, often to return home only having earned enough to pay the store rent. My mother needed the few odd pennies my sisters and I contributed to purchase food for the family. Otherwise, we didn't even know where our next meal was coming from.

Shy though I was, I knew that I had to advertise. I can still hear myself shouting bravely, "Hey, get your ice-cold soda here!" When we were very young our mother had taught my siblings and me that if we behaved and were very good, God would grant our wishes, assuming that they were simple and reasonable. Like: "Please, God, let the Yanks beat Boston in a doubleheader" or "Please, God, let me pass the math test even though I didn't study enough." And more often than not, He did seem to grant my wishes. And so if the sodas were selling slowly and the hours were dragging on, if I found myself becoming apprehensive I would whisper this simple prayer: "Please, God, just twenty-four bottles; make the ice last."

The Apple of My Eye   8

Mickey

It was one of those memorable conversations in the fall of 1972. We were expecting our second child in November and were discussing possible names. As we considered girls' names, Penina, her mother, Rebecca, and I savored the opportunity to name the baby Miriam, after Rebecca's mother. Miriam had died a decade earlier, but she did not yet have a child named after her. Penina's father, Ben, said little until we had concluded our discussion. Then, very quietly, he spoke one short sentence. "I know a name—Esther." As soon as he spoke, we knew that Esther would be part of the baby's name, if it were to be a girl. Ben's mother was well known to us, even though we had never met her, never spent a Shabbat with her, never seen her talk to her son. The story of her life had been passed down from one generation to another.

Ben was her only surviving child. His birth was a miracle to her after many miscarriages and stillbirths. She had been so frightened that he too might die that she decided to fool the angel of death by not speaking to her child for the first year of his life. Much to Esther's delight, Ben grew up to be a healthy boy. He lived with his mother and stepfather in Warsaw after his father, who had left for New York, had sent his wife a *get* (Jewish divorce). Many years later, when Ben's father made arrangements for his son to join him in New York, the decision was made: The fifteen-year-old boy would leave his mother and home and venture on alone. Despite a perilous journey, he arrived in the United States in 1923. He found his father living with his second wife and three small children. The wife was suffering from some form of mental illness, and the house was crowded and chaotic. It became clear that he could not stay there for any length of time, so Ben moved to a boardinghouse that accommodated young immigrants who had no other place to live. From then until he married Rebecca ten years later, Ben lived the life of an orphan.

When Ben left Warsaw, his mother must have known that she might never see him again. So it was. While Ben thought of her often and actually saved money for a return visit to Poland, the trip never materialized. His father borrowed the money for some investment and never returned the hard-saved cost of a ticket. Ben's mother and stepfather, like hundreds of thousands of other Jews, were rounded up by the Nazis in the 1940s and imprisoned in the Warsaw ghetto, shut away to die from starvation or disease. Sitting around the table in Elizabeth, New Jersey thirty years later, we all knew Esther deserved to have a great-grandchild named in her memory. We also knew how happy this would make Ben.

Jessica never much liked her Hebrew name, Esther, which became her middle name in English, but somehow she caught the spirit of Queen Esther, the Jewish heroine who saved her people by her beauty, wit, and fearless determination. These characteristics showed up time and again as Jess was growing up.

When Jess was about three years old, she developed her first crush. She definitely had good taste. The object of her affections was Andrew Schamess, then a grown-up and sophisticated thirteen-year-old son of our very good friends. It was common practice for the Schamess and Glazer families to have dinner together on Wednesday evenings at the Davis Student Center at Smith College. There, Jess could follow Andrew around, laugh at all his jokes, and charm him with her three-year-old antics. The trouble began when she learned to dial phone numbers. Once she knew the Schamess number, she would regularly call Andrew and keep him on the phone for a little chat. Finally, Penina and I told her that she was not allowed to call him anymore. After all, he was a big kid with friends his own age. One day, as I was walking upstairs, I heard some talking from the study. There I found Jess on the phone, whispering. "Andrew," she was saying, "I can't talk too long. My parents don't want me to call you anymore." Fortunately for her future husband Doug, Jess later turned to boys her own age, but she always retained a soft spot for Andrew.

On a trip across country when Jess was six years old, we could see more of her personality emerging. We all loved traveling through the West that summer, visiting national parks and other scenic areas. We arrived at Yosemite Park late one afternoon, just in time to move into one of the tent cabins in Curry Village. We rushed through dinner to get to the special viewing spot for the spectacular sunsets. As the sun went down, many of the visitors boarded the double-decker buses that would drop people off at the various areas of the park. We had driven over, but Josh and Jess begged to return to Curry Village on one of the buses. We found the correct one and told the driver we would wait for the kids at the designated stop.

They never arrived. We waited a half hour, becoming ever more anxious. By now it was almost dark. Finally a bus did appear, but there were no children. One of the passengers asked if we were the parents of the two youngsters who had boarded with him. He told us that the bus had broken down en route and that passengers were dispersed to other vehicles. He had tried to watch for them but lost them in the crowd. Now we were really worried. We spoke to a ranger and asked for advice. He thought we might check with the main information desk in Yosemite Village.

Just as it was becoming pitch black, we decided to return to our tent before going to security. Then, from behind the tent area, we heard some familiar voices. Josh and Jess suddenly appeared. They had boarded the wrong bus, and the driver told them he would let them off at the rear of Curry Village, and they could make their way back. Jess was really scared. Josh took her hand and told her not to worry. "I will take you back to the tent to meet Mom and Dad. "By the way," he asked her, "do you happen to remember our tent address?" There were hundreds of tent cabins, and they all looked identical—especially in the dark. "Of course," she answered, "ours is R-44." "Oh," he replied, "don't worry about a thing. I can get us back easily." And so it happened. This was so typical of both of them. Josh had the courage and the calmness, and Jessica had the memory and presence of mind to notice the number of the tent. This small incident became symbolic of their relationship for many years into the future. Jess always had complete trust that Josh could help her deal with a problem, and she could always provide the necessary details to make that come true.

Despite the usual sibling squabbling and Josh's ability to tease Jess mercilessly and evoke the most bloodcurdling screams from her, their bonds of solidarity continued to grow. In part, this was facilitated by their mutual love of the Boston Red Sox and the New England Patriots. Penina and I always believed that, as a little girl, Jess observed the sports enthusiasm that Josh and I shared. Consciously or not, as a very young child she determined to become part of our intimate circle and became an enthusiastic and knowledgeable sports fan. Her former housemate, Dinita, recalled evenings when a group of friends would gather to watch a Red Sox game. The guys would invariably attempt to put the girls down by touting their superior knowledge of the team. It worked, Dinita said, unless Jess was there. Then, her facility with the facts and her recall of controversial decisions evened the sides. They rarely could stump her, and she could always call her brother or her father to fill in any gaps in her knowledge.

If Jess wasn't born a committed feminist and a determined liberal, she must have developed those values as a very young girl. As long as I can remember, she would become irate if she heard sexist or racist comments. When she grew up and moved away, she called often. If she asked for me, we knew she had a sports question or story to tell;

if she asked to speak to Penina, it was often because of a feminist issue that arose at work or that she read about. She could discuss her political views with either or both of us. After she married, she made sure that she educated Doug to share her views, introducing him to Bill Maher and John Stewart to back up her ideas with pithy humor. Doug was open to all this, but alas, she could never turn him into a Red Sox or Patriots fan. Their sports rivalry lives on, and their little son Justin owns as much Miami Dolphins paraphernalia as he does that of the Red Sox or Patriots.

In 1985 when my father was eighty-eight years old, he became terminally ill. As he was admitted to the hospital, the dietician spoke to him about the meals. He was determined to be cooperative and maintained his charm to the end. "Whatever you say, sweetheart," were the last words that we heard him speak. Pa's stay in the hospital lasted six weeks, and he was in a coma for much of the time.

At one point during his hospitalization, Jessica, then twelve years old, indicated that she wanted to visit Pa. While they were of different generations and life experiences, she, like Josh and his other grandchildren, had developed a loving relationship with my father. Now it was time to say goodbye. Josh did not want to see Pa in this condition. He was clear that he wanted to remember his grandfather as the man who had sung him Yiddish songs and lullabies from the time he was born.

We were somewhat dubious about Jess's wish to visit Pa in the hospital. He was very sick, connected to all kinds of tubes, and not speaking. We were concerned that she would be upset to see him so ill. Jess was so insistent that we raised the issue with our friend Mike Perlman, a highly respected psychiatrist in Northampton, our hometown. He had known Jess for most of her life. Mike suggested that we respect Jessica's wishes and allow her to visit her grandfather. "Just make sure she understands she can change her mind up to the very last moment. She can go as far as the doorway to his room and then decide not to enter." She understood.

We arrived at the beginning of the visiting hours. There was no nurse on duty to raise questions about Jess's age. We both entered the room, stood on either side of the bed, and reached down to hold Pa's hand. Someone on the hospital staff had shaved my father and removed all the tubes. He looked calm and asleep. I didn't feel anything but the warmth of his touch, but Jessica felt him squeeze her hand. It was so meaningful to her. She spoke softly and reminded him of who she was. She did not seem tense at all. We talked about the visit long after it was over. She recounted her feelings of satisfaction that she had accomplished her mission, and that made her feel close to him. She had done what she thought was right and was her own person in making that decision.

Jessica was willing to confront the unpleasant facts of life with a can-do attitude. Unlike many children of our friends and acquaintances, she enjoyed working more than she liked school activities. So it was that just after graduating from high school in 1991, she decided to take a year off before starting college. She had a job in the cash office of the local Stop & Shop supermarket. In order to support the cost of an apartment that she had rented with a friend, she took a second part-time job at the Hotel Northampton. To do this, she needed some adjustment in her Stop & Shop schedule. When she spoke to the store manager, Mr. Ryan, about her request, he refused to accommodate her. This tall and imposing man looked down at her and told her that he wasn't about to give up the flexibility of determining her hours as he saw fit.

Jessica spoke to us about her predicament and her desire to seek the intervention of the union to which she had belonged since she had begun to work in the supermarket as a cashier at age 15. Under union rules, Mr. Ryan was required to meet her request. We cautioned her that while she was right in her interpretation of the rules, Mr. Ryan could easily retaliate and make her life miserable in a thousand ways. We explained that this was common practice in many companies, and we had seen it repeatedly in the scores of whistleblower cases that we had studied. We wanted to protect her from such an unpleasant fate and to be sure that she understood that there was a great power imbalance between a part-time clerk and the store's general manager.

Jess listened carefully as we discussed case after case. I could see she was impressed with the seriousness of our argument. She was not unfamiliar with our research. Over several years we had discussed many cases with her and Josh. Yet she would not be put off. "What's the point of belonging to a union if you can't go there for help just when you need it?" Penina and I backed off. As parents we felt very protective, yet we could not ignore the significance of her response. Though only eighteen years old, she was prepared to confront some of the realities of the world of work.

The outcome? Jess went to the union and, as a result, Mr. Ryan changed his mind and agreed to modify her schedule, which lasted for the remainder of the year. The next fall she began her studies at the University of Massachusetts in Amherst and transferred to a Stop & Shop closer to the campus. She didn't like the new location and wanted to resume work in the Northampton store, so she applied to return to her old job. Now Mr. Ryan had his chance for revenge. He was not obligated to take her back, and we felt quite certain that he would remember that she had gone over his head to the union and would simply deny her request. To our surprise, he did nothing of the sort. Maybe he realized that she had been a very good worker and was in fact quite loyal to Stop & Shop. Whatever his thinking, to his credit he agreed to her return. So much for our advice. Jess's position that she could stand up for her rights was vindicated. While she clearly internalized the values and ideas of her parents, she maintained her own positions and emerged with her values intact.

The teaching never goes only from parents to children. We all benefit from the wisdom of our kids, and I was no exception. Take, for example, an incident that happened when we were travelling in the Southwest and stopped at a Holiday Inn near a Navajo reservation. For several days I had been grumbling about the food that we found in restaurants in that area. On our last day there, we decided to have lunch at the Holiday Inn restaurant and order simple food. I requested a tuna fish sandwich, assuming that would be a safe choice. When a watery and unappetizing sandwich arrived, I was ready to tell the waiter that it was unacceptable. Jess saw what was coming and decided, at age eight, to intervene. She leaned forward across the table. "Dad," she said, "if there is one more complaint on this trip, when we get home there will be no milk and cookies for a week." Okay, I had been warned.

My Mother Never Worked   9

Itzik

My parents were married for more than sixty years, and every time they had an argument about money, my father would hurl these words at my mother: "A *vaybs arbet iz keyn arbet nisht.*" A woman's work isn't work. He must have said that hundreds of times.

And he was right! After all, she didn't earn any money; she brought no cash into the house. As we struggled through the Depression, he was convinced that the burden of keeping us alive fell squarely on his shoulders. To make matters worse, one fine day in 1934, my mother announced that she was pregnant. My two sisters and I were shocked. How could she do this to us? Her response to our expressions of anxiety over having another mouth to feed was not reassuring. She exclaimed, "Six can starve as cheaply as five!"

My mother was a responsible woman and always tried to help however she could, but she never actually worked. She struggled every day to keep herself busy so that she wouldn't be bored just hanging out. She seemed to find a lot of unimportant things to do. I remember that when I awoke each morning, my mother was already dressed and bustling. Our tiny, four-room apartment, which was heated by a coal stove in the kitchen, was warm. How did that happen? My mother must have attended to that early each morning. She helped me select the day's clothing from my "vast" assortment of hand-me-downs. Then she invited all of us to sit down and eat the breakfast that she had prepared for us.

My baby brother, having already been fed and changed, sat contentedly in his high chair while Mom made lunch for my sisters and me: a sandwich, a piece of fruit, and a cookie when we could afford it.

As we left for school, I could hear her breathe a sigh of relief. All she had to do now was help my father get off to work. When this simple chore was done, the day belonged to her. She and the baby could do whatever they wanted to do. She certainly didn't have to work, lucky her! Well, okay, maybe a little. She washed and dried the breakfast dishes and put them away—just for the fun of it, if you know what I mean.

I guess she made the beds too. They were always made by the time we returned from school. And yes, the apartment was always spotlessly clean. She must have done that as well. I know my sisters and I didn't do it. Well, even if Mom did it, how long could that have taken? Since she didn't work, she might as well have occupied her time doing something. And she had the whole day to do it. Come to think of it, on those rare occasions when I came home for lunch, I caught her listening to the radio, which, it seems to me, proves my point.

Wait now, let me think. Maybe she did have other ways to keep busy. We didn't own a washing machine—our clothes were always washed by hand. They were cleaned, pressed, and starched to perfection. In her spare time, she must have done that as well. This was before television, and since she didn't know how to read, she had nothing else to do.

On the other hand, because we had a tiny icebox, not a refrigerator, and very little money, she needed to go shopping for food every day. There were no supermarkets in our neighborhood, so she was forced to go to the greengrocer, the kosher butcher, the grocery store, and even the variety store. Bringing the bundles home from five or six blocks away, then dragging them and the baby up two flights of stairs

—how long could that take? And don't forget, she had to be home in time to greet us when we returned from school each day.

She would say, "Change your clothes, put on your sneakers, and have a glass of milk before you run down to play. And make sure you come up in time to do your homework before supper." Homework had to be done before supper because our desk was the kitchen table and school evenings were reserved for listening to our favorite radio programs. I would race out of the house to play ball for two hours.

And what was she doing during the time when I was so busy? Nothing! Well, almost nothing. She prepared supper for the family. First, for the four children, at about six o'clock. A little preparation: cooking, serving, cleaning up, putting things away, and then putting the baby to sleep. She never sat and ate with us, but she would serve us constantly, while she herself ate only intermittently.

Two hours later, when my father came home from his real job, he was served his dinner and she cleaned up for a second time. Then, finally, she was free to do whatever she pleased, at about nine thirty each night.

Wait a minute, I almost forgot. There were a few last-minute preparations for the next day: choosing our clothes, deciding what to make for lunch. And then she could sit down, relax, listen to the radio—and do the family mending. And then she was really done for the day. No, in fact, sometimes she might decide at the last minute to wash out a few things. But, in any case, by ten or eleven o'clock every night, she was definitely done.

So you see, she was a very lucky woman, my mother. She was supported throughout her married life by my father. She never had to work, not a single day, in her whole life. Her only job was to be the cook, maid, housekeeper, laundress, handyman, seamstress, psychologist, mediator, negotiator, arbitrator, doctor, dentist, pharmacist, guidance counselor, teacher, religious leader, accountant, lawyer, peacemaker, diplomat, politician, and general miracle worker. We gave her very little help or, rather, she would accept very little help from us. I would offer to run an errand if she'd forgotten eggs or onions or whatever. My sisters were willing to help clean the house, but they couldn't do it well enough to please her. As for my father in those pre–Women's Movement days: since woman's work was not work anyway, what reason was there for him to lift a finger around the house?

Now, whenever I think back to that time more than fifty years ago, when we were so young and perhaps a bit thoughtless, my father's words repeat in my mind: "A woman's work is not work." And the same response always comes back: Work? How could she have found the time? She was much too busy to work.

Harry Bredemeier –
a favorite teacher and mentor

Mickey and his friend Michel in Cleveland, 1958

Mickey and his social work buddies in the Air National Guard, 1958

PART FOUR

Old Friends & Good People

Mrs. Youshak   10

Itzik

He was very old and, unfortunately, a terrible nuisance. My family lived on the second floor of a three-story walk-up on Hegeman Avenue, and the old man and his wife occupied the front apartment on the ground floor. I had to pass their door on my way upstairs and that was a problem.

Many times, when he heard someone passing by, the old man would open his door suddenly and, without warning, begin to flail at me with both hands as I attempted to rush past. Usually, he was able to get in a few painful blows. When he hit me, I would complain to my mother.

My mother, being more understanding, always said, "Listen to me: he's very old and senile. He doesn't mean any harm. He doesn't know what he's doing. Try to walk quietly so he won't hear you. That way, he won't open his door." While I was successful most of the time, I found this recurring experience very annoying. So when I heard he had died, I suppose I was relieved, although I would have been ashamed to admit it. A few weeks later, my mother told us the old man's wife had moved away to live with a daughter in another city. Shortly thereafter, Mr. and Mrs. Youshak moved into the vacant apartment on the ground floor and changed our lives forever.

* * * * *

They were a strange couple—strange to us, at least. They were Jewish, but unlike any Jews we had ever met. They were Sephardic. They spoke a language called Ladino, not Yiddish. When they spoke English, it was with difficulty. And unlike the broken English spoken by my father, theirs had a Spanish flavor to it. They attended a synagogue whose service was different from ours and ate food unlike anything my mother ever prepared. They even looked different. They shared the complexion of people from the Mediterranean region.

At first, we exchanged brief hellos as we passed in the hall or on the street. But Mrs. Youshak was a warm, friendly person whose feelings were not to be denied. She insinuated her way into my mother's hectic life by insisting on being her friend. We learned from my mother that the Youshaks had been married for many years and yet were childless. I remember overhearing my mother whispering to my older sisters, "Women's trouble." I didn't know what that meant, but I knew I shouldn't ask.

Mrs. Youshak was a short, stocky woman with an olive complexion and jet-black hair. My mother often said, "She must have been a beautiful girl." Mr. Youshak was a good-looking, tall, heavyset, quiet man always dressed in a shirt and tie, which gave him the look of a prosperous executive. He was given to long periods of silence and seemed morose at times. Occasionally, when his wife displeased him, he would suddenly come alive and we would hear a rapid outburst of scolding in Ladino. Thanks to her gift for compromise, she soon placated him and when peace was restored, he would once again sit quietly for hours in their small living room, just staring out the window.

Due to poor health, Mr. Youshak was unable to keep a regular job and was unemployed for long periods of time. We learned that the Youshaks were "on relief," a phrase of the Depression years that preceded "on welfare.".Then, as now, "relief" entitled you to the barest necessities: some rent money, some money for food, and little else. No cars, telephones, vacations, or clothes. When Mr. Youshak did get a job for a short period of time, it was usually working for a relative for a few dollars a week as a night watchman in a small, neighborhood factory.

At that time, my friends and I used to play punchball all day in the backyard of our small apartment building. When Mr. Youshak was working nights, Mrs. Youshak would open her kitchen window, stick her head out, and say in a quiet voice filled with both pleading and expectation, "Itsikl, darling, Mr. Youshak is sleeping. Please play outside so he can sleep. He's not feeling well and he's working nights now." Whenever she called out to me, never challenging or demanding, my response was always the same. Since I was the unofficial leader of the gang of players, I would shout, "Okay, guys. We have to play outside now." And off we'd march, out of the yard.

For years afterward, whenever we'd meet, particularly if other people were with us, Mrs. Youshak would tell that story in great detail. "So I would open the window and call out to my Itsikl, my child [she always called me and my brother and sisters her children] to play outside, and always, always, he and his friends would leave so Mr. Youshak could sleep."

As I entered my adolescence, that story always embarrassed me because she told it with such delight and love. "My Itsikl," she would say, and if I was close by she would kiss me and add, "an angel. My own children…."

Neither I nor anyone else could refuse her simple requests. I would meet her occasionally on New Lots Avenue, the main shopping area of our neighborhood, and stop and listen as she spoke in a mixture of Ladino and English to the local greengrocer. I was intrigued. What did she ask for? Rotting vegetables. She always went there at the end of the business day to ask for rotting vegetables, the things they would throw out before the next business day began. In her gentle, almost timid, way, she would offer to buy them for a few pennies. At times, if the vegetables were "too far gone," barely salvageable, they would be given to her for free. If they still could be sold, she was offered them at a fraction of their original price. I would stand there and watch as the business deal was consummated.

Later that day, when I would pass her door on my way upstairs, I would pause momentarily to inhale the strange and intoxicating aromas of the mysterious foods she was preparing. The hall smelled of exotic delights cooked with unknown spices and herbs. I would think of the damaged, forlorn-looking vegetables that she had bought and marvel at her magic that transformed those "has-beens" into a gourmet meal.

At times, when we had even less to eat than the Youshaks, she would offer to share her food with our family. My mother would always protest, but she would finally accept only to feed her hungry children. When this happened, we would have an exotic feast unlike anything my mother had ever prepared. And since people like us never went to a restaurant, this food provided a welcome change.

Being "on relief" meant periodically having to deal with the relief bureaucracy. Although Mrs. Youshak could barely read and write English, she had the courage of a lion. She refused to be intimidated by politicians, agencies, or bureaucrats. She would sit and argue, never accepting their reasons for why she wasn't entitled to the small favors she asked. On many occasions, she returned home to delight us with stories of her encounters with the "forces of evil." She would tell us how, even with her limited command of English, she had managed to soften the heart of a bureaucrat who had agreed to some request that went slightly beyond his understanding of "the rules." She had learned to play their game.

During one particularly painful period in our lives when my father earned nothing from his printing business on Sutter Avenue, Mrs. Youshak decided to call the New York City relief agency to tell them of our plight: we had no food, no money, and were threatened with being dispossessed from our apartment. The social worker at the relief agency listened to her story of a proud family who refused to ask for help and agreed to send an investigator. When Mrs. Youshak told my mother what she had done, my mother accepted the offer only "to feed her four children."

I remember the morning the investigator arrived. She knocked at the door. When she walked in, she saw a tiny, spotlessly clean apartment. We were all adequately dressed, thanks to our hand-me-down clothes. My mother invited the investigator to sit down, offered her a glass of tea, which she politely refused, and the very brief interview began.

The investigator asked our name, inquired about our family composition, asked some questions that my mother answered honestly, and then the interview ended abruptly. The woman asked my mother: "Your husband is at work?" "Yes." "He has a store?" "Yes."

"Madam, there are starving families in New York City whose husbands do not work at all." The investigator rose and snapped her briefcase closed. "Thanks for wasting my time," she said as she left. How could we expect an investigator to believe that my father had a business that enabled us to starve with amazing regularity? Thank goodness we didn't have to explain that he had a broken-down old car that he needed for his business. That was the last time my family ever sought any assistance from a city agency.

Having learned to cope with the bureaucratic forces, Mrs. Youshak intimated that there was one more hurdle she had to overcome. She dreamed of becoming an American citizen. Her husband had become a citizen and she stubbornly planned to accomplish this wondrous feat. This proved to be her hardest endeavor. She could read English...a little. She could write English...a little. She spoke English...after a fashion. But if desire was the deciding factor, we knew she would succeed. She studied very hard. My sisters and I helped her and cheered her on.

Finally the day of the hearing arrived. Mrs. Youshak asked my oldest sister Fay to accompany her to the city. When they returned several hours later, my sister regaled us with an account of Mrs.

Youshak's performance at the hearing. She told us word for word what had taken place. We imagined the scene at the immigration department:

Interviewer: Now, Mrs. Youshak, please tell us the name of the first president of the United States.

Mrs. Youshak: A wonderful man, good-looking, on a beautiful horse. His name was "the Father of Our Country," he lived in Mount Vernon, he was married to Martha Washington. His name was George. From Virginia, right. Helped win the war, right. A wonderful man.

Interviewer: What is the Fourth of July?

Mrs. Youshak: Hot, usually very hot. A hot Independence Day.

Interviewer: Can the United States Constitution be changed?

Mrs. Youshak: Okay, yes.

If she knew the answer to a question, she included every detail she could remember. So when the interviewer asked her the name of the national anthem, Mrs. Youshak stood up and began to sing "The Star-Spangled Banner"! At that point, the interview was considered over.

My sister sat quietly by as Mrs. Youshak answered all the questions. We never were certain but, knowing Mrs. Youshak, we were sure she had charmed them into giving her citizenship. Who could refuse this wonderful creature? She would be an asset to any country.

As the years passed, all of our lives changed dramatically. In 1943, I left to serve in the U.S. Army and was away for two and a half years. In 1945, my father's business improved dramatically, and my parents moved from Hegeman Avenue to a better neighborhood and a larger apartment, two miles away. My two sisters married and moved away to start their own families. Some years later, my brother and I both married and moved away. Our news of the Youshaks now came from bulletins my mother provided us.

We were a close-knit family and we never forgot the many kindnesses that Mrs. Youshak had bestowed upon us through the years. One spring, while we were visiting our parents, my mother informed us that the Youshaks were in declining health and had hoped to spend the summer away from the city heat at a small bungalow in the Rockaways. Of course, they didn't have the money to pay for it. So my mother suggested that we all contribute a share to pay for the cost of the vacation. I can proudly say that without hesitation we all volunteered the necessary sum and the Youshaks spent the summer at the beach.

Mrs. Youshak, my mother informed us, tearfully extolled the virtues of her "good children" for their generosity. Ironically, this episode caused an unforeseen problem. Months later, my mother called to say that Mr. Youshak's brother, who grudgingly gave them a few dollars from time to time, was furious that they had money for a summer vacation and accused them of having a cache they had never told him about. The story that Mrs. Glasser's children, strangers and not relatives, had given them the money was more than he would believe. Therefore, he threatened to withhold the little help that he did usually offer them. My mother tried to explain to him why we had given them this gift. And while he was probably never fully convinced, he did withdraw his threats. He certainly didn't understand what Mrs. Youshak meant to my mother, who told us many times, even to the point of embarrassing us, that she felt closer to Mrs. Youshak than to her own three sisters.

Some years passed and we heard that Mr. Youshak had finally succumbed to one of his many ailments. Mrs. Youshak, by now older and frailer, had chosen to move to a nursing home for Sephardic Jews somewhere in Bensonhurst. We visited her there from time to time, always talking about our sweet, though often painful, shared experiences on Hegeman Avenue ... the "good old days," when we were all younger. During one such visit Mrs. Youshak recalled to us how, many years before, she had often listened to my father walking the floor in the middle of the night, carrying the new baby, singing strange and funny nonsense songs as he attempted to lull him back to sleep. We smiled at being reminded of that experience.

When it was time to leave we would always promise to return for another visit very soon. But we were so busy with our own young and growing families that the visits became less and less frequent. And then, one day, my mother called to tell us that when she phoned the nursing home to speak to Mrs. Youshak, she was told that Mrs. Youshak had died several weeks earlier. Her relatives had not even bothered to inform us of Mrs. Youshak's death or to invite us to the funeral.

Mrs. Youshak, *du blaybst in undzer lebn*. You remain in our lives, in our hearts, and in our memories. You gave us precious gifts. You taught us sharing, even when there was little to share. You taught us the true meaning of charity. And above all, you enriched our lives with your love. Along with our parents, you set an example for us of what we hoped to become.

Just an Ordinary Man   11

Mickey

When I was studying at Rutgers, I went to one particularly memorable Shabbat dinner. My friend Liz had invited all the participants in the Rutgers–Douglass sociology seminar to her parents' home one fall Friday night. The seminar participants included several Douglass seniors and seven graduate students, most of whom were not Jewish. The Enrights were quite religious and took Shabbat very seriously. Mrs. Enright prepared a traditional meal, which included home-baked challah, chopped liver, chicken soup, and roasted chicken, complete with baked potatoes. The food tasted as good as it smelled when we walked in the door. As a curious sociologist, my friend Larry Karachi from Kenosha, Wisconsin, asked an array of questions about our hosts' beliefs and practices. Larry had never been to a Shabbat dinner before, and he was particularly interested to learn how Orthodox Jews lived up to their high ethical standards. As part of this conversation, Mr. Enright told us about his work rescuing orphans after the war. It was a dramatic story, and we were totally captivated by his account.

Liz's father, a local businessman in Elizabeth, New Jersey, had taken an active interest in European children orphaned by the Nazis' murderous policies. While 1,500,000 children had perished in the ghettos and concentration camps, thousands of others survived and were sent to displaced persons camps throughout Europe. They had been traumatized by their experiences and struggled to resurrect lives with the help of Jewish organizations. At the camps, the children were provided with care until they could resettle in either the United States or Palestine (which became the State of Israel in 1948). Despite all the good intentions, many were still living in limbo years after the war had ended. Mr. Enright felt responsible for their plight. He had the compassion and the resources to undertake his own rescue mission. Periodically, he flew to Europe, went to the DP camps, and arranged for orphaned children to be resettled with Orthodox Jewish families in the New Jersey area.

On one of those trips, he returned home with one of the children, who became a third daughter in his family. Given how much Orthodox Jews value sons, the community was very surprised that Mr. Enright, the father of two daughters, had not chosen to adopt a little boy for himself. Surely there were many boys waiting for good homes. But Mr. Enright explained, with a statement that always brings tears to my eyes, "You see, whenever I came to the camp, there was a beautiful little girl waiting for me at the gate. I became attached to the four-year-old Judy with the dark eyes and beautiful smile. She reminded me of the preciousness of childhood. I just could not leave her there."

Judy's health had been seriously compromised by years of war and neglect. Doctors recommended that she might thrive in the drier climate of Arizona. So the Enrights packed up the family and moved there for a year, until Judy's health improved. To this day, I can still see her in the camera of my eye, by then a lovely teenager standing and davening in the women's section of the Elizabeth shul.

I met Mr. Enright only that one evening in 1958. Yet, I remember that night so vividly. Perhaps it was the modest way he told the story and the fact that he did not feel that he had done anything extraordinary. His story seemed to embody the wisdom that came from one of the most famous sayings in "The Ethics of the Fathers": "It is not incumbent upon you to complete the work of repairing the world, but neither are you at liberty to desist from it."

In the Best of Company   12

Mickey

In 1956, just after graduating from City College of New York, I enrolled in the School of Applied Social Sciences (SASS), a social work program at Case Western Reserve University. It was there that I met Michel Wasserberger, an older student from France. Michel had been awarded a scholarship to study in the United States for one year in recognition of his outstanding work as director of a boys' home in Paris for children who had been orphaned during the war. Unlike most of the other students, who had come to graduate study directly from their undergraduate programs, Michel had a longer and more complicated history. He had been born in Hungary in 1914, had moved to Paris in the 1930s, and had joined the French army after the Germans invaded France. Michel was captured and spent several months in a German prisoner of war camp before escaping. He claimed that he escaped by climbing out of a toilet window. He was a big man, and I wondered how he had maneuvered out of such a small space. He reassured me that it was possible. "Where your head goes, your *tush* can also follow." Michel then joined the French Resistance. He successfully avoided arrest by the Germans, knowing full well that if he were captured, he would be executed as an escaped POW, as a member of the Resistance, and most assuredly as a foreign Jew.

In retrospect, I am astounded by my hesitancy in raising more probing questions about his experiences. Since then I have learned that 1 million Frenchmen served as prisoners of war in Germany, performing labor in the factories and fields. Among them, the Jews were often singled out for "special treatment." We now know that 75,000 of the Jews who came to France from other countries were deported to the death camps. Why didn't I ask about that? In the period immediately after 1945, discussions about the Holocaust were relatively rare in the United States, France, and even Israel. A veil of silence cloaked the horrors of what had transpired in the ghettos and camps, and many of those affected believed that it was better to forget and move on with one's life. But Michel was not a man to bury unpleasant truths. I have to believe that my own lack of sustained questions is explained by the strong culture among the social work students to focus all our energies on our mission in the here and now. But perhaps Michel's impact on me was subtler than I realized at the time. For within a very few years I was deeply influenced by my reading of Raul Hilberg's *The Destruction of the European Jews*, a pioneering work in Holocaust scholarship. Maybe Michel unknowingly prepared me, his future housemate, for a lifetime of teaching and studying about resistance to evil.

With the defeat of the Nazis and the liberation of France, Michel began a lifelong work with orphan boys in a Jewish agency. As soon as I met him, I recognized the extraordinary quality of the man. I was twenty years his junior and admired his good sense and his experience in dealing with youth and others. To me he seemed so much wiser than the social work teachers with whom we were studying. They emphasized that the strict requirements of professionalism mandated that social workers maintain a clearly drawn distance from their clients. "Detached concern" seemed a hallmark of their approach. Michel had worked for years with traumatized boys who had survived the Holocaust and who had lost their families and their childhoods. He found the obsession with professional detachment misplaced when his charges needed emotional connection in order to heal and rebuild their lives. He valued the historical and social context over the Freudian approach so favored by most faculty at the school.

Despite the tension between Michel and his professors, I strongly urged him to stay for a second year. He applied and received permission and funding to complete the master's degree. When that yearlong extension was granted, Michel and I rented an apartment together several miles from the school.

Michel had a wonderful sense of humor and a homespun philosophy that always lifted my spirits. During the Thanksgiving break, I went off to Michigan to visit my cousin Bert. When I returned I found Michel in a morose mood. "Mickey," he said, "it is good to have you home. When I was younger and alone, I knew that I was in the best of company. But now, at age forty-three, I am not so sure. Welcome back." At another time, after a visit to a dentist, he shared the following devastating thought. "Mickey, to lose a lover is very sad. To lose your teeth is a tragedy."

Michel's influence expanded to include my eating habits. As a waiter in a hotel in the Catskill Mountains during the summer, I had grown to hate chicken after the cook had served it to the wait staff every night for ten weeks. I had vowed never to eat it again. Despite Michel's urging, I refused to try his roasted chicken. Slowly, over a period of weeks, I became ever more attracted to his cooking because of the relish with which he approached his meals. The aroma, the chewing, and the sense of enjoyment he felt were palpable. I thought perhaps, just perhaps, I should reconsider my boycott of chicken. When I finally broke down and tried it, much to his delight, I loved his cooking.

As my relationship with Michel blossomed, my studies at SASS faltered. My academic work continued to show promise, but my field placement was less successful. In the first year, I had worked with middle-class families who were adopting foster children, and that was fine. My second-year placement was in a social welfare agency.

My level of experience and maturity faced a more stringent test there. One of my clients was a schizophrenic woman whose life seemed totally out of control. When I entered her apartment it was chaotic, filled with books and papers and food everywhere, unlike anything I had ever seen. Another client was a young, single, African-American woman, with four very small children, whose despair was evident. I remember thinking that my brother Itz and sister-in-law Estelle were so occupied with their new baby, and there were two of them and they had a regular income. How could I ever help these desperate clients to cope with their situations? We had an ideology of creating a better world but, with the tools at our disposal, I did not see much possibility for improving the lives of these desperately poor and troubled people.

I told Michel of my feelings of inadequacy in relating to these women. He urged me to remain calm and not expect too much of myself too quickly. He emphasized how much he had learned over time in order to relate effectively to the orphan children in France. He had found that it was important to focus on listening to the children relate their experiences and help them make sense of their stories. The orphans he worked with needed his constant attention and his belief in the possibility of a brighter future that lay before them. Despite their loss of family and years of brutality, they could recover. He told me that the children's experiences were often well beyond his own, making it challenging for him to empathize and establish boundaries at the same time. He encouraged me to believe that I could provide concrete help to my needy clients and offer them some hope.

Despite Michel's supportive words, the fieldwork remained very difficult. I began to think maybe my talents lay in other areas, such as teaching or research. I decided, after much agonizing, to drop out of the program and enroll in several graduate courses in history and sociology. I felt a deep sense of loss at leaving my SASS group. In my year and a half in Cleveland I had developed an array of warm friendships. We were a close group who not only studied together but also socialized at parties, movies, concerts, and even on the softball field. We had formed bonds that were strengthened by a shared mission to contribute to a better world. I know these values were tinged with a bit of romanticism, but we definitely believed in the possibility of a more compassionate society. It was very painful to cut myself off from all of that. But, as difficult as it was to do at the time, it turned out to be a life-changing and very wise decision.

After receiving his degree, Michel traveled in the States for a few months and then returned to France to his position as director of the boys' home. At the same time, when it seemed almost certain that I would be drafted into the army, I joined the Air National Guard with several SASS friends. The Guard required a summer of basic training at Lackland Air Force Base in San Antonio, Texas. At the conclusion of our basic training, our commitment was to one weekend a month of service, which allowed me to join a new academic program as a full-time graduate student. While still in Cleveland, I had noticed an announcement of a new offering at Rutgers University that seemed made to order for me. They were starting a master's degree in applied sociology, with a paid research internship at a state prison. I applied and, much to my delight, was accepted. The following September I found myself in New Brunswick, on my way to a promising career as a sociology teacher and researcher. Of course, there was another, unanticipated bonus in New Jersey, because that is where I fell in love with Penina.

More than three decades later, in 1992, Penina and I spent a week in Paris after doing research in Prague. I was determined to find Michel, although we had lost contact over the years. I was eager to tell him that my plan had been successful. I had found the kind of work I had been searching for and the woman who became my lifelong partner. I knew Michel would be so happy to know I had two wonderful children.

As soon as we were settled in the hotel, I looked in the Paris phone book, and there was his name. I dialed his number with great anticipation and introduced myself to his wife when she answered the phone. Irma immediately recalled all the stories Michel had told her about me and about our time together as roommates. After a few minutes of pleasant conversation, I asked her if I could speak to Michel. "Oh, no," she said, "Michel died fifteen years ago." I was totally unprepared for this shocking news. Irma made plans to meet with Penina and me and to return several letters that I had written to Michel. One was a particularly emotional response to a letter that I had received from him when I was still in basic training. He had not heard from me and feared that I had forgotten about him. I remember so clearly that when I read that letter, I began to cry. In the reply that Irma had kept, I apologized for not writing sooner and vowed that I had not forgotten my old friend and I never would. But somehow we had not stayed in touch, and now it was too late. He was gone.

I had so many questions to ask him. How did he evaluate the benefits of his studies in the United States? Had he brought renewed knowledge, energy, and insights to his work as school director? How did he respond to the changes in French society as a result of World War II? How did he react to anti-Semitic outbursts that punctuated life in France? What did he think about Israel's growth into a Middle East power?

I imagined the four of us, Michel, Irma, Penina, and me, drinking wine and eating excellent food in Michel's favorite café. I thought of how, as we rekindled our friendship, I would impress Michel with my progress from social work dropout to Ph.D. in sociology from Princeton University. I was keen for him to know that I had made good use of my social work training in my research and teaching. I had learned to listen with special care both to students and to those I interviewed. I wanted to tell him about my research in Chile, where I raised sensitive political issues with university students and was subsequently accused of being an agent for the CIA. I would have talked to him about teaching sociology and my focus on ethical issues, and I would have told him that Penina and I had written several books together about people of courage.

I know Michel would have listened intently and, with friendly pride, would have raised provocative questions, so reminiscent of the long discussions we had when we shared an apartment in Cleveland many years earlier. Toward the end of our time together he would have taken me aside to praise my choice of a wife. "Mickey," he would have said, with his arm around my shoulder, "you are a lucky man." How I missed that quiet, intimate exchange. Perhaps it is sufficient if, only in my imagination, this was the last gift from my Paris friend.

PART FIVE

Facing Our Demons

The Cellar 13

Itzik

"The only thing we have to fear is fear itself." President Franklin Delano Roosevelt made that statement in his first inaugural address on March 4th, 1933. It was easy for him to say. He didn't live in a small, crowded apartment with a musty, "dangerous" cellar.

At the time the president said that, the greatest form of pleasure for my siblings and me was listening to the radio. The radio happily took us into the twenty-fifth century with Buck Rogers and all his interplanetary companions. It transported us to the Old West, where justice was meted out at the end of a six-shooter as the Lone Ranger and his faithful companion Tonto rode everywhere, righting wrongs. At the end of each chapter the Lone Ranger turned culprits over to the inept—but always grateful—local sheriff before riding off with a hearty "Hi-yo Silver, the Lone Ranger rides again." I listened faithfully every Monday, Wednesday, and Friday.

However, most thrilling but scariest were the mystery programs. Titles such as "The Witches Tale," "Lights Out," "Inner Sanctum," and "The Shadow" delighted and terrorized us once each week with a new horror story. With the use of fine actors and brilliant sound effects, they created an atmosphere in our minds that no movie or television could achieve.

After the weekly eerie introduction, we were transported in seconds onto the moors of Scotland, as whip-crazed horses pulling a dark and ominous looking carriage approached a castle. In our minds, we saw a flash of lightning followed by a clap of thunder, which seemed to spell impending doom. The unsuspecting passengers inside the carriage spoke flippantly about rumors of the castle being haunted. The ghosts, we were told, were the murdered relatives seeking revenge before they could go to their eternal resting place.

When the driver finally arrived at his destination, the occupants disembarked and the trunks and suitcases were unloaded. The nervous driver was paid, whipped the horses, and was gone. From this moment on, the listeners, mostly young fools like me, sat in stunned silence as we heard, and saw in our mind's eye, the weary travelers unlock the rusty old doors. With candles in hand, they entered their new home. (Why they always had to arrive at night, in the rain, was something I couldn't understand.) For the next thirty minutes, we were treated to the clanking of invisible chains and the moans of ancestors long dead. For no apparent reason, windows would blow open, suddenly extinguishing the candles, as our heroine emitted the first of several piercing screams. Her foolishly brave fiancé would immediately assure her that everything was fine. As the story continued to unfold, we were treated to walls that turned when you leaned against a statue, passageways that led to dark dungeons below, and inexplicable sounds of ghosts floating by. You can readily understand how the president's words had a particularly special meaning for me.

My problem was that our apartment was heated by a coal stove in the kitchen. During the cold winter months, it was someone's responsibility to get the coal. My mother assigned that job to me. She insisted that since I was the oldest boy and didn't help clean the house, I had to perform other chores, such as running errands and getting the coal.

Because of the mystery shows on the radio, I lived in constant fear from adventure to adventure, from week to week. I regularly promised myself that I would stop listening to these wild tales, but I was addicted. I tried every trick, used every maneuver, made up outlandish excuses, and attempted various ploys. I was hoping to have someone take turns with me when the agonizing trip to the cellar was necessary. I hated the thought of having to do it every day.

In the evening, often just after I had finished listening to one of my favorite mystery stories, my mother would ask me to bring up a bucket of coal from the cellar. Easy, right? Wrong! I usually made the trip with a horrific story fresh in my mind. I was ashamed to mention this to the members of my family, for they would surely laugh at my wild imagination.

"It's a cellar, just a cellar. What are you talking about? So it's dark. So what if there are shadows on the walls. Mice? Maybe. Water bugs? A few. So what else?" How could I tell them that the cellar was my haunted castle?

I was gratified when, years later, my sisters admitted to me that on the rare occasion when they went down into the cellar, they too went with great apprehension. It was a scary place. The dark corners, creaking of the ceiling above, and muffled voices would alarm any sensible person with an imagination.

Oh, with what reluctance I would pick up the coal bucket each night and start for the door. I would stop and make one last desperate play to avoid making the trip, at least for one night. Suddenly, I would begin walking with a limp.

"What is it?" my mother would ask with concern.

"My leg, my leg. I've sprained my leg. I can't walk!"

"Wait, I'll get you a crutch. Go down and bring up the coal."

Or else I pretended that I couldn't move an arm. "My arm, my arm, it's paralyzed!"

"Carry the pail with the other hand. Go down and bring up the coal."

I even complained of sudden blindness.

"Wait," my mother said. "Here, I'll give you a dime."

"It's only a penny," I complained when she handed it to me.

"Nu," she said, "I'll owe you nine cents. See how much your eyesight has improved! Stop being blind. Go down and bring up the coal!"

One final, feeble try. "Mom, my appendix hurts. Can somebody else get the coal tonight?"

"All right, we'll send Mickey. Mickey, wake up. Get out of your crib. I'll change your diaper and you'll bring up the coal tonight."

My sisters would howl with laughter, and my mother would say "*Mamzer*, go down and bring up the coal!"

The battle was lost. I would pick up the bucket, walk out of the apartment, and trudge down the stairs. The first leg of the journey was easy. The cellar entrance was on the ground floor at the back of our house. The hall was dimly lit, but it did not alarm me. But the cellar! As I approached the cellar door, I was seized by a cold fear. What terrifying adventure lay before me? The choice was not mine. I had to go. I approached the door slowly, with extreme caution and even greater trepidation. I unlocked it. What dangers awaited me on the other side the moment I removed the lock? I opened the heavy wooden door and peered down below into the darkness while I reached for the switch that lighted the first set of stairs to the cellar below. Suddenly, as I flipped the switch, the stairwell was aglow with the extraordinary brightness that only a fifteen-watt bulb can provide. A dark haze brightened this dismal area. The stairs creaked painfully as I descended, one hesitant step at a time, into that catacomb to await my fate on the landing below, while my mind played back the eerie sound effects of a recent radio episode. To my fertile imagination, the cellar began to change into a haunted castle. I was carrying a lantern instead of a flashlight. I was dressed in eighteenth-century English garb.

Coal bucket in one hand and flashlight in the other as weapons, I made my way to the basement floor. Another weak bulb on the landing below provided the balance of light for the entire basement.

Spread out before me were several blind spots, labyrinths, dungeons, and secret passageways, all perfect hiding places from which my assailant could launch an attack. Invisible bats flew past my unprotected head.

How well I remember those imaginary encounters in the cellar. The troubling shadows cast on the walls were my enemies. There in a corner stood a man with a peg leg, sword in hand. Up on the ceiling an enormous spider, awakened by the clanking of my coal bucket, began to creep from his web toward me. Hands seemed to reach from all directions, trying to grab me as I dodged out of the way. An old coat tree standing erect seemed to be pointing at me, ordering my destruction. My mind surrendered completely to fantasies. What were the assorted sounds, occasional screams, muffled cries, and conspiratorial whispers? Were they garbled voices from apartments above, or from the demons surrounding me? With a sense of foreboding, I slowly turned the corner. Ahead of me stood the locked bins, one belonging to each tenant. What did they contain? Were they locked securely? Could something spring out and attack me? Our coal bin lay at the very back. I walked noiselessly to an area that was becoming increasingly dark.

As I approached the bins, I pushed the button on the flashlight and prayed that it would stay lit for the few moments I needed for my task. The flashlight performed in its usual feeble way, alternating between little light and less light, but it worked. When I reached our bin, I took another key from my pocket and slowly removed the lock. Opening it, I peered inside carefully. No monsters, gangsters, witches, Martians. Only coal and a small coal shovel. Quickly I filled the bucket with coal, scoop after scoop, periodically glancing over my shoulder. I realized that if I was being hunted, I was trapped in the back with no possible escape route, and I prayed that "they" wouldn't get me.

Moments later, the bucket was full. I threw down the shovel, removed the bucket, now heavy with coal, placed it outside the bin, and, with trembling hands, locked the door, looking about to make sure that I was still alone. I lifted the bucket and backed my way along the dark passageway as quickly as I could to the safety of the stairwell, shining the flashlight over the floor, walls, and ceiling as I went.

Reaching the end of the passageway, I turned to climb the stairs. As I shut off the downstairs light, the area was thrown into total darkness. I knew that I had to complete my escape before it was too late. Once upstairs, I put down the bucket, shut the stairwell light, and locked the door in one swift motion. I breathed a great sigh of relief, for I had made it once again without being kidnapped, captured, tortured, or held for ransom.

"Mrs. Glasser, we've got your son Irving. If you ever want to see him alive again, bring seventy-five cents in unmarked coins, small denominations, to 1451 Pitkin Avenue by five o'clock tomorrow." Well, it could happen.

I walked up the flight of stairs to our apartment and went inside. Depositing the coal bucket near the stove, I replaced the flashlight in the kitchen drawer and sat down in front of the radio. It was almost time to listen to one of my favorite mysteries, "Inner Sanctum" a tense tale featuring squealing doors, rain-swept nights, eerie sounds, and mysterious basements filled with a labyrinth of rooms, dark and forbidding dancing shadows, spiderwebs, and hidden passageways leading to who-knew-where. Once again, the magic of these shows would take hold of me.

Occasionally, when my nightly chore was completed and the radio program was finished, my courage would reassert itself. I was thankful once again to be in the bosom of my family, and I would become playful. I would shut off all the lights in our apartment, remove the flashlight from the drawer, and stalk about the house, holding the flashlight under my chin to create an eerie glow. Moaning and groaning in a frightening way, I would try to scare my sisters, my little brother, and my mother, always with the same result. My mother would say, "*Nu*, stop acting like such a *meshugene*."

Dinner for Four in Paris   14

Mickey

I knew it was good news when I heard the phone message to call Penina. She told me that our paper on environmental crusaders had been accepted for the next meeting of the International Sociological Society in Paris in August 1994. It would be our second trip to Paris. We had loved the first visit and often reminisced about our long walks throughout the city, the outstanding museums, and the wonderful dinners we had in the small, unpretentious bistros. Once again, we made reservations at Grandes Ecoles, a charming hotel on the Left Bank. Our second trip turned out to be even more exciting, but not in the ways we had anticipated. Rather, we had an unexpected meeting that evoked memories of a distant past when I was a young and struggling graduate student at a crossroad in my career.

As I entered the large reception room on the opening day of the conference, I was delighted to see John W. Riley, a former professor of mine, who had played a pivotal role in launching my sociology career. Riley had been chairman of the Rutgers University Sociology Department in the 1950s, and under his leadership the department had created a new master's degree program in applied sociology. I had been one of seven people invited to join the first graduate class, and this acceptance allowed me to withdraw from social work school with an ambitious and exciting plan for the future, albeit with some trepidation.

I remember receiving the registered letter from Professor Riley that detailed the terms of the appointment, including a paid internship at Trenton State Prison to do research on inmate recidivism. Working within the walls of a maximum-security prison would be a totally new and challenging experience for me. The letter also specified that, as members of the first cohort of graduate students, we were invited to participate in department meetings to help plan other aspects of the graduate program. This was a true vote of confidence bestowed on our small, untried group. It was a remarkable opportunity, not usually given to first-year graduate students, to be part of the inner workings of an academic department. I remember feeling a debt of gratitude toward Jack Riley. He had placed his credibility on the line with university administrators and with some members of his own department in order to convince them that he could effectively fund and staff this program.

The offer was perfect for me. My previous semester in Cleveland had been quite difficult. I had dropped out of social work school at Case Western Reserve University and was unsure of how to move forward until I saw the announcement of the innovative program at Rutgers. I was still sad at leaving my social work friends and harboring some doubts about where this new master's program would lead me. But it was reassuring to move closer to my family and friends in New York City and start over in graduate school. As I prepared for the move, I rented a two-room, basement apartment in a private house near the campus. I had never lived alone before, and I wanted to define this experience as part of a new adventure.

Although I had always admired him, Jack Riley and I had not been particularly close during my Rutgers years, and I had seen him only a very few times after leaving New Brunswick. Now, some thirty-five years later, we found ourselves at the same conference in Paris. I was unprepared for the warmth of his welcome. He was a senior member of the conference planning committee, so it was natural for him to be among the official greeters. Yet his approach to me was anything but formal or prescribed. His handshake and embrace were of the kind usually reserved for special friends or colleagues. Within a few moments he had his arm around me and was introducing me as one of his first and most prized students. He emphasized that I had helped build the Rutgers graduate program many years earlier.

It was clear from his comments, as he introduced me, that he had followed my career and research and was proud that I had carved a path in the sociological study of ethical and courageous behavior. I was gratified and somewhat amused. I remembered his informal assessment of my potential many years earlier, when I was still a Rutgers student. Riley, a strictly quantitative researcher, had once said, "Mickey, I see you as a future first-rate teacher. I don't yet see you as a particularly productive researcher." He was half right. Working with large data sets and big stacks of IBM cards, the fashion at the time, was not my forte. I needed to find the type of research that played to my strengths and my sociological imagination. I began that journey at Rutgers and continued refining my interviewing and qualitative research skills throughout my studies. Now, thirty-five years later, Jack Riley was celebrating the results that came from my devotion to developing my own path.

Jack was so enthusiastic about my work that I was somewhat unsure of who was garnering all the credit—I, or the Rutgers sociology program for its wisdom in selecting me. Frankly, I didn't care. I knew at that moment that Jack Riley, a man I liked and respected, was holding me up as a symbol of the department's success. I had justified his imagination and all his hard work. And, indeed, he was right. Rutgers had played a crucial role in starting me on my life's work.

But there was more than just a warm greeting. Jack told me that the conference planners had given him and his wife Matilda far too many francs to spend. He insisted that Penina and I join them for dinner, and we suggested a wonderful fish restaurant only a few blocks from the hotel. As we started out, Jack asked if I could do him a favor and allow him to lean on my arm. As I felt the pressure of his hand,

I remembered that I had been impressed by his stature and stamina thirty years earlier. Now in his eighties, he was more vulnerable, and he sought my help. It was there for the asking. As Jack took my arm, he plied me with questions about our family and about the research that Penina and I had completed together, which reminded him of the work that he and Matilda had coauthored over so many years. While somewhat frail in body and gait, he was still strong in mind and spirit. So it was that the four of us embarked on a delightful evening of walking, eating, drinking good wine, and talking.

Why did Jack Riley's warm overtures matter so much to me? After all, at that time I was at the height of my professional career. I was a full professor at Smith College and a well-regarded teacher. Penina and I had published several books, including our study on whistleblowers just a few years earlier. The book had been very well received and even had been toasted by several members of Congress across the political spectrum. We were so proud when U.S. Congresswoman Barbara Boxer spoke at a congressional reception in honor of the book. At the time of our dinner with the Rileys we were deeply involved in our study of community activists. We had already interviewed people in the United States, Israel, and Czechoslovakia and were finishing the manuscript that would soon become The Environmental Crusaders.

I was happy to share some of this history with Jack and Matilda. At the same time, the dinner with the Rileys reawakened many questions from my past. I remembered my fear of failure that was a remnant of my dropping out of social work school. But most of all, I realized at that dinner just how important the Rutgers program had been in serving as a transition from my aborted social work career to my future as a sociology professor and researcher. It was a memory of a vulnerable period in my life that I thought I had put behind me. Strangely, it had risen to the surface in this most congenial surrounding.

My thoughts drifted to my very first face-to-face meeting with Jack. In that early discussion with him in his office in the sociology building, he sensed that I still bore some scars from leaving Western Reserve. He assured me that the faculty adviser there had written a strong letter of support. Jack emphasized that whatever challenges I had confronted in Cleveland would not affect my research and writing in sociology. After all, I had excelled in the academic subjects there but struggled, as a twenty-two-year-old, with the clinical demands of the program. This focus on addressing and resolving clients' problems, Riley emphasized, was simply not part of academic sociology. His vote of confidence that very first week helped put some of my anxieties to rest.

A few days later was the first meeting of the "magnificent seven," as we new graduate students humorously labeled ourselves. Jack Riley spelled out in detail why each of us had been selected. The department admissions committee had chosen a group with diverse backgrounds, skills, and even temperaments. He thought that we could teach one another effectively—and no doubt inform the faculty as well. Although we enjoyed all the compliments, our group always teased each other: If we were the elite of all the applicants, what in God's name did the rejects look like? Laughter served as a tonic, easing the inevitable fears that graduate students experience.

At the dinner in Paris, Jack asked about my life after leaving Rutgers. He particularly wanted to know, even so many years later, whether the Rutgers program had effectively prepared me for my Ph.D. studies at Princeton. I told him about several crucial faculty members with whom I had studied. In my first semester at Rutgers I met the best professor I ever encountered. Harry Bredemeier was a master teacher. He challenged undergraduate and graduate students alike to ponder difficult questions about fundamental societal issues. I remember how exhausted, yet exhilarated, I felt leaving his class after each meeting. I knew I wanted to be a teacher like him—challenging, insightful, and imaginative. It was in his seminar that I came to appreciate sociology as an intellectual endeavor. Harry served as my model in years to come. He became a mentor, then a colleague and friend for the rest of his life.

I told Jack that his program had been crucial to my future in another way. In my second year, through a Rutgers faculty member, I secured a position as a research assistant in the Industrial Relations Section at Princeton University. I was delighted to be part of that academic group. I met and worked with faculty and students who encouraged me to apply to the Sociology Department at Princeton for admission into its Ph.D. program. And this, of course, changed my life. My relationship with members of the Industrial Relations Section influenced my work throughout my thesis research on Chilean university students and well beyond. Without attending the Rutgers program, I never would have been admitted to Princeton. It would not even have occurred to me to apply.

I realize now, looking back on that evening in Paris, that it was more than just an elderly teacher praising a former student. Just as I was indebted to Jack for creating the new and experimental program in applied sociology, so was he indebted to me and the other graduate students for our subsequent professional successes. Our accomplishments affirmed for him the program's usefulness and contributions to the field. He felt that he had left a lasting legacy.

My meeting with Jack was an encounter of shared emotions. He, in his eighties and of diminished health, took special pleasure in showing off his younger colleague to his peers. He was boastful the way teachers can be when they meet former students who have justified their life's work. Just as I had trusted him years ago to guide me and watch out for my interests, so he now felt confident that I would adjust my stride to his as we walked along those Paris streets. With Penina and Matilda walking ahead of us as our guides, Jack and I felt secure that we were going in the right direction.

Mickey's Years in Brooklyn

Mickey and his two oldest nephews –
David and Larry

Mickey and his Mother, Ida

Itz reading

Itz's audience

Itz and Estelle

Cousin Molly was the arbiter of family taste

Our Families Expand

Paul and Gosha

Jess and Doug

Danny and Michele

Ruth and Ken

Josh and Tamar

Our Parents' Wedding

Ida and Nathan sixty years later with their youngest grandchildren – Josh and Jessica

PART SIX

Dangerous Journeys

Going to the Country   15

Itzik

My father never owned a car during the 1930s. To hear him tell it, he owned several junk boxes, a few *tarabaykes*, several lemons, and untold aggravation-mobiles. He was never able to sell his cars because by the time he bought them, they were already fit for the scrap heap. He used to brag that every car he bought was guaranteed for the life of the car or thirty days, whichever came first. He would spend twenty-five, fifty, or seventy-five dollars with reckless abandon, for that was all he could afford at the time.

Each car entered and left our lives with amazing regularity, and we mourned none of them. We were always happy to see them move on to a better life in that great, big junkyard in the sky. And while his cars were all capable of transporting him from our apartment to his store and back again, a distance of at least four miles, they were not built for longer trips. Herein lay the problem.

Our yearly trips "to the country," the Catskills, always proved to be high adventure. We knew when we wanted to start out. We even knew when we hoped to arrive. But from the moment my father started the engine and pulled away from the curb until we entered the parking lot of the Kenoza Lake Country Club, outside of Monticello, New York, our trek was fraught with horrific incidents that made us respect the early settlers who traversed the United States to a new home thousands of miles away. Every problem they had, we had. In fact, in some ways they were better off—their horses were more reliable than our cars. Imagine if we'd been under attack from hostile natives—warriors on horseback would have easily outraced us!

The New York State Thruway had not yet been built. That meant traveling up old Route 17 through small, sleepy towns that did not particularly care for the yearly migration of city dwellers disturbing their quiet life. We had to be wary of speed traps: if you were doing twenty miles an hour in a fifteen-miles-an-hour zone, the unfriendly local police were happy to treat you as a source of income for the town or themselves.

The mandatory yearly stop at a roadside rest called Miller's 666, halfway to our destination, was not for us to eat or to use the toilet facilities, but to allow the car to rest. Believe me, the car needed it. With its six, seven, or eight passengers and with suitcases on the riders' laps, in the small trunk, tied to the roof, and even strapped to the sides, the car was usually exhausted by the time we sighted the Miller's sign. This stop was similar to emergency surgery at any metropolitan hospital. My father was the chief surgeon. "Okay, raise the hood so she can breathe. Don't stand too close. Give her air. Check the radiator. How do the tires look?"

The team of doctors issued its diagnosis: the car was overheated. (So what else was new?) She couldn't climb hills. (Hello! Could you, with six or more fat *zhlobs* riding on your back?) The tires were worn. (So? We all had holes in our shoes.) The battery was weak; the horn didn't work. Thank God the motor knocked; at least we knew the engine was still alive.

"Will she make it?" we asked my father. "*Me darf leybn mit ofening!* [Let's hope!] If we get there [not when we get there], she'll rest for a few days before we ask her to drive us home." Thinking back now, I know it must be my imagination, but when we stopped, I swear that I heard the car *krekhts*, or moan.

As we set off on the second part of our journey, when we had traveled a few miles from Miller's, someone would finally dare to utter the phrase that each year struck terror into our hearts: "So what do you think? Will it make the Wurtsboro hill?" This hill was the last obstacle standing between us and a few pleasant days away from the noise and heat of the city.

The Wurtsboro hill was a long climb into the mountains that, when crossed, led us to our Shangri-la. One year, the car was loaded with our family and several members of my father's business partner's family, a number of robust journeymen (each member of the family weighing in at about sixteen stone—and believe me, they were big, heavy stones). The car began to climb the Wurtsburo hill, and after a few feeble moments it belched, coughed, prayed, and finally stopped. The car seemed to say, "I think I can, I think I can, I think I can … I can't."

"The car is trying to tell us something," my father said. "Everybody out. I'm afraid we'll have to do this in two shifts. Two skinny people and two fat people for each trip." And that day, that was how we crossed the mountain to the great Catskill land beyond. It took much longer, but we made it. Normal driving time for the 120-mile trip was always four to eight or ten hours, allowing for breakdowns, overheating, tire changing, repairs, and rest stops—all for the car.

On another occasion, I recall my father trying an experiment he had heard of, one that others had performed with success. It worked: he backed up the Wurtsboro hill.

One summer, we were going to spend a week at Kenoza Lake with the Rabinowitzes, my father's partner's family. Which car would we use? Our undependable car, or theirs, which was equally undependable but a year younger? Joe Rabinowitz volunteered his family's car as the lesser of two evils and, unfortunately, my father agreed.

By the time the car was loaded with eight bodies and we had all climbed aboard, once again, every conceivable space—the front, the back, the sides, the trunk, and the roof—was completely filled. As we pulled away from the curb, one of our neighbors shouted after us, "Don't bother making the trip—there's no work in California, Mr. Joad!"

The idea was to start out at one o'clock and get to the hotel in plenty of time for dinner at seven. At first, the trip was uneventful. We left Brooklyn, crossed into Manhattan, taking the West Side Highway north to the newly opened George Washington Bridge. From there onto Route 4 leading to Route 17 and the Catskill Mountains, with our usual stop for rest and relaxation, for the car, at Miller's 666. Once we reached Route 17, we were in the country. Anyplace that had grass and trees was the country to us.

We had our first of three flats as we entered New Jersey—the tires weren't used to fresh air. Okay; we changed the tire, fixed the flat, and were off again. The trip to Miller's took about four hours and our dinner was now in jeopardy. So what? The kitchen was open late; we would find something to eat. Two more flats and an overheating, a hose replacement, and we were now ready to enter the last part of our journey as we watched, with some misgivings, the sun go down.

Dinner? Forget it. Let's just get there. And the last fifteen miles once again proved the resourcefulness of man. It was now time to turn on the headlights as we prayed that the car had the energy to finish the trip. Joe flicked the light switch on and the road was suddenly aglow with what seemed like the power of six birthday candles. We'd now entered a small, deserted, two-lane country road, the last leg of our journey. The car lights were sufficient to make out the outline of the car and the shadow of the trees on either side of the road.

Joe kept calm, announcing that if he drove very slowly, he could see the road well enough, and since there were no cliffs to go over and few dangerous ditches, we would get to the hotel without incident within two hours. And for the next hour and a half, we drove slowly; we inched forward carefully, stopping at every signpost to make sure we were on the right road, since the darkness had made us strangers to a route we had traveled many times in the past.

It was a harrowing experience for the adults and a scary but exhilarating adventure for the children. When we finally arrived at Kenoza Lake, at about eleven o'clock, my mother was in a state of hysterical agitation, and my father vowed that never again would he allow anyone to drive him to the country in a car more undependable than his own.

A Public and a Private Nuisance

15

Mickey

It all began for Penina and me in early 1961. My beloved 1950 Mercury was using more oil than gas, and we desperately needed a new car. But we were graduate students and had very little money. One day Arnie, a friend of Ayala and Yudi, (Penina's sister and brother-in-law) told us that he had just purchased a brand-new car for only $850. How was this possible? Even in those days, this was an amazingly cheap price. While the design seemed comparable to that of other European cars on the American market, such as the French Renault or Italian Fiat, there was a catch. The Skoda that Arnie purchased was virtually unsalable in the United States because the car had a fatal flaw. It was manufactured in Communist Czechoslovakia, and this was the height of the Cold War. No one but a fool or a desperate graduate student would buy a car made behind the Iron Curtain.

Nevertheless, we were intrigued by the possibility. We knew of Skoda steelworks, a Czech company that was productive and well-known before World War II. We thought they would make a good product, even if it was not politically correct. We decided to pursue the possibility and make an offer for the car. We also alerted our close friends, Steve and Carol DeMeritt, of this exceptional buy. Like us, they were graduate students living on the cheap. Steve and I contacted the Skoda dealer in Manhattan and set forth to fetch our prize.

For years after, Steve reminded me of my great negotiating skills. The dealer asked for $850 for the car, but I told him that we would take two cars for a better price. Don't ask me how it happened, but we ended up paying $1725 for two cars. The dealer must have laughed all the way to the bank.

The extra $25 turned out to be the least of our problems. Steve and I were guilty of gross naïveté. We never carefully inspected the car. Only later did we realize that, had we done so, we would have seen that every rubber hose in the car was rotted and cracked, and that might have been a clue to the general quality. We also never asked how one would acquire replacement parts, should anything break. But we would find that out within a few short weeks.

As it turned out, I was not the main one to bear the brunt of the car's problems. Both Penina and I were enrolled in graduate school. My classes at Princeton were only a mile from where we lived. But she was attending Rutgers, which was fifteen miles away, and she needed to drive to school everyday. Driving Snorky the Skoda became a true test of Penina's driving skills, patience for endless mechanical problems, and calmness in the face of multiple breakdowns.

For the first few weeks, it was fun to drive a new car. Then, one day, Snorky would not start. The battery was dead, and the car was only a month old. A call to Carol and Steve revealed that they were experiencing the same problem. This kind of communication with the DeMeritts became a regular feature. It was like hearing the morning's weather forecast and sporting news. "Good morning, Carol. Don't count on your battery today. Ours is dead." Then there were the reports on the radiator, the starter, the engine valves, the carburetor, and the hoses. Who knew that a car could have so many parts go wrong?

We were able to replace the defective battery by purchasing another one. We did not need a special Skoda part. But other repairs took a much more ingenious response. Take the starter, for example. A few months after we had purchased the car, I was feeling pretty confident. Aside from the battery and a few hoses, not too much had gone wrong yet. I offered a friend a ride home from the library one day. I actually boasted to him about our good buy. Oh, the power of positive thinking. The starter was a knob, on the right side of the car. Given the cold temperature that day, I knew I would have to pull a little harder than usual to make sure the engine turned over. Suddenly, to my horror, the knob was in my hand and a hapless cable was hanging from the dashboard. I gasped out loud, "Oh, my God! What have I done?"

When I finally managed to get home, Penina tried to be reassuring by rationalizing what had happened. "After all," she said, "it wasn't really Snorky's fault. It's a very cold day, and any car might have had some difficulties." That led to an important distinction in our house—between things that were Snorky's fault and things that were not.

The knob that fell off was only the tip of the iceberg. Within a few short weeks, the whole starter system went *kaput*. After much searching, we found a mechanic who specialized in foreign cars and deigned to try to work on our lowly Skoda. Penina drove the car a half hour to Somerville, New Jersey, to the auto repair shop. As the mechanic began tinkering with the malfunctioning starter, the whole thing ignited and was burning under the hood. He calmly turned to Penina and said, "Should I let it go? Then you will be rid of this headache." Was she foolish to decline his offer or worried about how we would manage without any car at all? Whatever her reasons, she prevailed upon him to extinguish the fire and proceed with the repair. For years to come, as she faced a variety of difficult decisions, she would say, "Do I have the guts to let the whole thing burn?"

Naturally, the mechanic could not repair a burnt-out starter. He had to call the New York mafia and try to find a replacement part. That would take about two weeks, if we were lucky. So he gave the car a small push that turned over the engine, and Penina drove home to report on her first adventure of driving without a starter. Look!

Snorky was a small, four-cylinder car with a manual transmission, and it wasn't hard for a few people to push from the rear with the car in neutral to jump-start it. So that's what we did for the next two weeks. Our friend Bob Cook was a fellow graduate student living in our housing project. He was very strong and had even been the New Jersey state weight-lifting champion. Every morning he came over; Penina sat in the driver's seat, and he and I pushed the car until we heard that satisfying sound of the engine's purr. You would have been hard pressed to call it a roaring engine. Poor Snorky was very delicate. My brother Itz used to say that it was the only car he knew where you would have to downshift into second to go over a cigarette butt. But, with a push or two, the car actually started, so Penina took off for New Brunswick, hoping to park on a corner where there was a small slope. At the end of the day she would roll the car down the hill and let the engine kick in. If that failed, she stood on the Rutgers campus waiting for some kind student to come and give her a small push. As for me, as soon as I saw her take off, I picked up my books and walked over to the magnificent Firestone Library on the Princeton campus. It was a tough life.

By Friday, Penina was truly exhausted from the events of the week. So she innocently turned and said to me, "Why don't we go to Elizabeth and have Shabbat dinner with my parents? It will be a nice break." I was horrified. "Are you crazy? I am not driving to Elizabeth in a car that doesn't have a starter." As I spoke, I slowly realized I had made a big mistake. I tried to recoup by explaining that we both had had difficult weeks; surely Penina needed to rest, and we would go to Elizabeth another time soon.

True to my word, we decided to head for the Migdals' home about two weeks later. The starter had been fixed, and our little chariot was off and running. It was a nasty, rainy evening, but that didn't bother us. Until… why was the needle on the dashboard moving farther and farther to the right? Was the car overheating? No, that could not be. But, of course, poor Snorky had sprung a big leak in the radiator, and the water was gushing out faster than we could replace it. So every fifteen minutes I got out of the car in the pouring rain and added water to the radiator. Penina, self-satisfied, refused to get out of the car. Her excuse was that she would keep the engine going while I administered the life-sustaining liquids. She did suggest driving with the hood up; that way the rain could pour directly into the radiator. Believe me, I was tempted. We arrived at Elizabeth cold, wet, and hungry. It took an excellent meal and some coaxing by Penina's parents to get us back into a good mood.

All of this was small potatoes compared to the time Penina broke down on the highway between Princeton and New Brunswick. She phoned me to say that something was definitely wrong with the car. She was in an Esso gas station and would try to limp on home. My friend, Mike Lewis, and I were visiting Bob and Karin Cook. I became increasingly anxious as we waited and waited for Penina's return. An hour passed with no word. Finally, as it was getting dark, I kept imagining her sitting on the side of Route 1, desperate to contact me. Karin suggested that we go and look for her. So Bob, Mike, and I piled into Bob's car and set off on Route 1. We kept looking at the cars speeding by on the other side of the highway, but of course it was dark and impossible to spot our Skoda. At one point Mike said, "I think that's the car across the highway." Bob made a quick U-turn and began chasing the vehicle. But, of course, it wasn't Snorky at all. So we turned around and kept driving. Then we arrived at the Esso station. It was dark and locked up, with no sign of Penina or the Skoda. Where was she? Dejected and worried, we headed back to Princeton, not sure what to do next.

When we drove up to the graduate student housing projects, there was the car parked in front of our house. The lights were on, and I breathed a big sigh of relief. We raced in to find out what had happened. I was a nervous wreck, but Penina was quite calm. As the car conked out, she explained, she had managed to pull it over into a gas station. The people there directed her to the back of the building, where a couple of mechanics had a small repair shop, not visible from the highway. There she found two Italian immigrants preparing to close up for the night. When they saw her desperation, they agreed to look at the car. "You are missing a gasket," they explained, "and that's the source of your problem." Oh, God! she thought. Not another two-week wait to order a part. "Don't worry," they assured her. "In Italy, during the war, there was tremendous scarcity, and we could never get parts. So we know how to make everything." True to their word, they custom-made a gasket, fixed the car, and an hour later she was on her way. It was a very low-tech operation in a small shop with no telephone to contact me. Penina was awestruck at the competence and ingenuity of these two men and thrilled at her luck in finding them. Ironically, she had experienced a great cross-cultural adventure, while I had imagined her lying in a ditch on the side of the road. Our friend, Mike, listened to the whole story. "You all know," he said, "that my father was an official in the Communist party, always on the run from McCarthyites. Nothing else could do it, but this car has finally transformed me into a fervent anti-Communist."

Don't think that Carol and Steve were sitting pretty all these times. Their Skoda was the first to need new valves for the engine, and Steve found yet another mechanic willing to meet us after-hours in his boss's garage to do some repairs. Steve had worked in a psychiatric center and was the first to figure out that our new savior was a pill-popping drug addict, as likely to do nothing and take our money as he was to actually repair the cars. After a while, the DeMeritts gave up all hope and parked their broken-down car on the street in front of the Rutgers graduate housing project. Eventually, a policeman came by and said they could not leave the car there with expired license plates. They were not sure how to get rid of their jalopy, so they ignored the policeman's directives. A few weeks later, he drove by again. "You know," he told them, "this car is a public nuisance." "You are completely right," said Steve. "It is also a private nuisance." The cop didn't get the joke, but we all thought it was hilarious.

Fast-forward to two years from the date of purchase. I had just been awarded a fellowship to travel to Chile for my doctoral research. Obviously, I had to sell the car as we prepared to be away for a year. I took the car to the mechanic near the Migdals' house, and he offered me $25. I accepted and was thrilled to be liberated. Penina's father was horrified. He could not believe I would sell a two-year-old car for $25, but I assured him it was I who got the bargain.

Remember Arnie, who first recommended the car? Do you want to know what happened to his Skoda? Well, Arnie was not a graduate student. I think he may never have gone to college. He saw the handwriting on the wall and sold his car one month after he purchased it. So much for the value of a good education.

All of the events described above actually happened to Penina and me. Somehow, our marriage survived, and our friendship with the DeMeritts flourished.

Itz's high school graduation

Itz in W.W. II

PART SEVEN
A New Identity

Falling Out of Love 17

Mickey

Seeing the recent film 42 was a wonderful experience. Both Penina and I admired Jackie Robinson, the first African-American player in the major leagues, and she even included him in a course on American history. The movie was a dramatic portrayal of his great triumph over race-baiting, cursing, spiking, and other threats by opposing teams. For baseball enthusiasts like the two of us, the evening was a total win–win experience. The good guy, helped and encouraged by Brooklyn Dodger team owner Branch Rickey and teammates such as Pee Wee Reese, emerged as a true American hero. Jackie was the kind of person you wanted to identify with.

At the same time, the experience raised some serious questions for me. How could I, as a teenager who cared about racial justice, not have rooted for Jackie Robinson? When my friends and I went to a game at Ebbets Field in Brooklyn, how could I have sat on my hands when all my friends were on their feet applauding when Jackie made a sparkling play at second base, bare-handing a ball that was headed for the outfield? I remember my best friend Burt asking me how I could be such a poor sport. The answer, lame as it seems now, two-thirds of a century later, is fairly simple. I was a dyed-in-the-wool Yankee fan, and the Dodgers were the enemy, part of a long-standing local rivalry.

Thinking about all this as we left the theater brought back a range of emotions. But let us not move so quickly forward. Let's go back to the early days when I first became a baseball fan, in 1947, the year Jackie Robinson reached the majors. Let's place the blame where it belongs. The villain of this piece is my much admired and loved older brother, Irving Martin Glasser. It was Itz, nine years older than I, who indoctrinated me into total love of the Yankees. Itz, who was normally a true radical with a leftist political orientation, was nonetheless attracted to the glamour of the Yankee pinstripes and their long succession of victories. The least a poor kid from Brooklyn could do was to identify with the winners, even though he grew up right in the heart of Dodgers territory. Although Itz left New York for several years, serving in the army in New Guinea, the Philippines, and Japan, he still remained unswervingly loyal to the Yankees.

Rooting for a team is not a rational thing, and the fact that the Dodgers were the first to racially integrate baseball was not sufficient reason for us to change our undying affection for the Yankees and their great players. The pull between our team loyalty and our other politics remained unresolved at the time.

The height of my love affair with the Yankees was in 1949. The Boston Red Sox came to Yankee stadium for the last two games of the regular season. They needed only one victory to clinch the pennant. The Red Sox quickly jumped out to a 4-0 lead, and it looked as if all were lost. In an act of desperation, the Yankees manager brought in their fabled closer, not in the usual ninth inning, but rather in the fifth—hoping that he could hold the Red Sox and allow his team to make a comeback. I can still hear the public address announcer's deep voice: "Your attention please. ladies and gentlemen. Now pitching for the Yankees, number 11—Joe Page." What a moment! Itz and I turned off the radio and went outside to play basketball with some friends. We could not bear to see the Yankees go down to defeat this way. A little while later, some friends signaled us that the game was tied, and we ran back upstairs just in time to see Johnny Lindell hit a home run to put the Yankees ahead for good. That turned the tide. The Yankees won that game and the next and were going to the World Series.

The first two games of the World Series each had a score of 1-0. The Yankees won the first game, and the Dodgers followed, with their only victory. Because the score was so close, it seemed all the more important to root against Robinson. My loyalty remained steadfast as the Yankees went on to win many other championships. What was so remarkable was that the teams seemed quite evenly matched and the Series often went to seven games. But the Yankees always seemed to be on the winning side. The Dodgers had their only World Series victory in 1955, shortly before they left Brooklyn for good in 1957.

That change coincided with my move to Cleveland and my waning interest in baseball. I was still a Yankees fan, but not of the same order. Roll the clock forward to 1959, when the hand of fate intervened, and I began dating a true Dodgers enthusiast. Who would have thought that the fans of two opposing teams could forge a long-term relationship? Somehow we managed. With the intensity of graduate school and going to South America for sixteen months, baseball became less important in our lives. Until the summer of 1967. We were spending the summer in Cambridge with Joel and his fiancée Marcy just as the city of Boston became consumed with baseball fever. After years of dismal records, the Boston Red Sox had come alive and were battling for a first-place finish in the American League. We could not resist the pennant fever that permeated the city. We went to our first game in Fenway Park, and all of us became Red Sox fans, at least for that time.

When Josh was born a few months later, Penina tried to convince me that we lived in New England and it was only right to bring up our children as Red Sox fans. I agreed, but I knew that deep down my heart was still with the Yankees, and I managed to live with this duality. Things changed in the late 1970s and early 80s when Billy Martin, the Yankees feisty manager, was in continuous battle with his boss, George Steinbrenner, who had a penchant for hiring and firing managers. Martin would get into some battle with one or more of the players, and Steinbrenner would dramatically fire him. And then the whole cycle would repeat itself. During one of those moments of turmoil, I realized that my loyalty to the Yankees had been completely undermined by their revolting behavior. My heart was no longer with them. I had fallen out of love. Much as Penina was pleased by the revelation that I was done with the Yankees, she did express some concern. "Are you telling me that I am living with a man who can fall out of love from one moment to the next?" I tried to tell her this estrangement had been building for some time. She was not completely reassured.

At that point, the four of us—Penina, Josh, Jess, and I—became rabid Red Sox fans, and boy, did we pay the price. In 2003, when the Red Sox lost a heartbreaking play-off game to the Yankees, we roamed the streets of Northampton at one in the morning, bemoaning our fate and far too aggravated to go to bed. A year later, in 2004, the tables were turned. Jess was in Florida, and Josh was on a research trip in Mississippi. Both were on the phone—first holding their breath and then elated as the Red Sox won their first World Series in eighty-six years.

As the years passed, our enthusiasm for the Red Sox continued. By the time we became Red Sox fans, there were some famous black players on the team. But a residue of racism permeated the team, which had been the last in the major leagues to hire a black player. We were grateful that a new ownership took over the team in 2004 and worked actively to combat the perception of racism that lingered over the decades. It was a lot easier to root for the team when whole segments of the Dominican community came out to cheer Pedro Martinez. This year, the team's greatest hero is its most dark-skinned player—the incomparable Big Papi.

For fans like us, some seasons were excellent—such as 2007, when the Red Sox again won the World Series. Some years were more disheartening, but none more so than 2012, when the team's terrible performance was matched by clubhouse infighting, a pugnacious manager, and an overall unpleasant atmosphere. I thought all winter about ending my love affair with baseball. The Red Sox had ended their season in last place. It was time, I thought, to make the break. The characteristics that I had most admired in the team—resilience, fortitude, energy, compassion, and fairness—now seemed to elude them. I thought this might be a strategic time to bail out. The aggravation was exceeding the pleasure.

On one of our long walks, I hesitantly broached the subject with Penina. I told her I was giving up the ghost. Predictably, she had another take on the issue. She put my decision in the context of my health and age and paraphrased the advice given to all seniors: Do not drop a central activity or interest in your life without adding another one. She reminded me that following the Red Sox meant having a lot of fun together. It was also a bond with our children. We enjoyed trying to outthink the manager and coaching staff, imagining trades and free agent signings. It was also a way to engage with many people around town, creating opportunities for everyday conversation with the custodians I knew at Smith College, workers at the recycling center, or even a stranger at the Florida beach who sported a Red Sox cap. It was easy to commiserate with these fellow fans when the team was losing and celebrate with high fives when the game went well.

Part of me knew Penina was right. This deep-seated ambivalence about my love for baseball went back a long way. I turned the clock back to more than a quarter century earlier, when my son Josh and I went to a game at Fenway Park. We got there early and stood in the spot where we had an excellent view of the pitcher warming up in the bullpen. We were mesmerized as we watched a young rookie throw one blazing fastball after another into the pocket of the catcher's mitt. In a moment of self-awareness, I turned to my eighteen-year-old son and asked, "What am I, a fifty-one-year-old professor, doing, watching this young kid showing his stuff? Without blinking an eye and never taking his gaze off Roger Clemens, Josh said, "Stick with it, Dad. This is great." "Oh," I answered rather profoundly, "I guess you're right," and we both continued watching, awestruck at the talent of the youngster below. "Josh," I asked, "do you think anyone can really hit that pitch?"

Now, so many years later, I am asking the same question. What is a man who has spent his life studying and teaching about profound problems of our century—from whistleblowers who fought for safety in nuclear plants to activists struggling against toxic waste dumps in their communities—what is he doing worrying about who will play first base and what the batting order should be? It's a fair question, but the answer is that maybe the disconnect is not so great. I can easily identify with the historian Doris Kearns Goodwin, who poignantly described her attitudes as a fan in a charming memoir. When writing a book, she said, she was never free from her work. Wherever she went, she was thinking about her research—with one exception. When she walked up the ramp and saw the grass in Fenway Park, then everything else disappeared. I know just what she means. It is a total release. As involved as I get in watching a game, as upset as I am at a stupid loss, as much as I rehash some of the plays, I still know at bottom that it's only a game. But boy, can it feel good. Can I tell you about the 2013 climb from worst to first, about Ortiz's grand slam when all seemed lost, and about Lester's extraordinary pitching? Well—maybe next time.

My First Real Job   18

Itzik

It was a cold November morning, not yet six o'clock, as I reluctantly walked up the short flight of stairs, entered that unfriendly office, and approached the desk, thinking to myself, what the hell am I doing here? I remembered with displeasure the four-month roller-coaster ride that had brought me here in the first place. I said to the man sitting behind the desk, when he looked up, "My name is Irving Glasser," a name that still sounded strange to me.

Four months earlier, on July 20, 1943, on my eighteenth birthday, I had done what every red-blooded American male did. With trepidation and serious misgivings, I reported to my local draft board to register for military service, a low paying, dangerous job with dubious prospects and an insecure future. This simple act changed my life for the next thirty-two months. It took me from the familiar and friendly streets of Brooklyn and sent me on a circuitous journey, covering more than forty thousand miles, to different parts of the country and world.

An argument ensued the moment I handed my birth certificate to the head of the draft board. He asked me my name and I said, "My name is Irving Glazer."

He looked at the birth certificate, looked up at me, and said, "It says Irving Glasser."

I had recently acquired a copy, since the original had been lost years before. I had never bothered to get a new one since I was sure I knew who I was.

He said, again, "Glasser" and I responded, "Glazer."

He said, "Glasser" and I insisted, "Glazer."

"Glasser."

"Glazer."

"Glazer."

"Glasser."

We sounded like the lyrics of an old Gershwin tune. He stated very simply, "We go by the birth certificate. Your name is Glasser!"

I thought to myself, not only don't I want to be here, but now I also have to walk around with an alias for the rest of my life. Great!

After I answered all the questions and filled out all the forms I was told to expect notification within a fortnight of where and when to report for my first physical examination. I was permitted to leave, with the admonition that I was tentatively a member of the armed forces in spite of my temporary civilian status. Oh, lucky me.

Sometime in August, I received a notice to report to a local hospital for a preliminary physical. Upon arriving there, I milled around with several hundred aspirants for the job of soldier or sailor. After waiting impatiently, we were each given a blood test and told to enter a large assembly room. There, a doctor announced from the podium that he was going to read off a list of diseases. Those of us who did not suffer from any of these were free to leave and would be notified by mail of our military classification. The rest of the group, those remaining behind, were to be examined further and disqualified at this juncture if their physical condition fell within the parameters indicated. At the end of the doctor's announcement, I left the room.

So it was that when I received a postcard a few days later listing my status as 4-F, I was in a state of shock. (4-F means that one is unfit for military duty.). Since I hadn't remained behind after the announcement, my logical conclusion was that the doctors had discovered that I had a serious blood disease.

My father and I went immediately to the draft board to demand an explanation. While I wasn't anxious to go off to war, to fight, to kill, or to be killed, even in a justifiable war as I believed this one to be, neither did I want the label "4-F" associated with me at this time of great patriotic fervor. The member of the draft board, understanding our concern, calmed us and offered to check the records and answer our questions. He walked to the files, extracted a folder, studied it, and announced without concern, "You're 4-F because you suffer from epilepsy."

A look of surprise crossed our faces. Could you determine epilepsy from a blood test? While I knew little of medicine, I thought not. I had never had any seizures or, for that matter, any other serious health problems. The whole thing didn't make any sense. We left the office suspecting that a mistake had been made.

My father, understanding my concern, said, "We'll visit a private doctor and see what he says." That afternoon a local doctor gave me a thorough examination and assured us that some error had been made. I felt somewhat reassured as we left his office, but my father, sensing that I was still troubled by the original diagnosis, suggested getting a second opinion. Later that afternoon, the second doctor confirmed what the first doctor had said, that I was in excellent health. He advised me not to worry but to enjoy my good fortune, get a job, and continue my education.

Within days I applied for a government job that didn't require a uniform; I was hired to work for the Veterans Administration, processing insurance claims. I registered for night classes at Brooklyn College, and my civilian future seemed happily in place.

For the next few weeks I was busy at work in Manhattan, having accepted, somewhat reluctantly, my position as a healthy 4-F. I looked forward to the beginning of the school year, and my girlfriend and I shared the joy of my staying at home. How easily we can rationalize. I decided that I would support the war effort by buying war bonds, saving tinfoil, which was used in the manufacture of weapons, and actively supporting the various rationing programs at that time. I certainly was prepared to do my share.

Imagine my surprise when, without any further examination or notification, I received a 1-A card (indicating my fitness for, and acceptance to, military service) in the mail. With mixed emotion, I remember being somewhat relieved that the error had been discovered. I could imagine some poor soul protesting that he had epilepsy and was not fit to serve, having a seizure in front of the members of the draft board to prove his point. Who knows, maybe his name was Irving Glazer.

I reported for my pre-induction physical at the Grand Central Terminal building. The scene, if it appeared on speeded-up film, would have looked like something right out of an old Charlie Chaplin movie. Total bedlam. Hundreds of men being "processed" every few minutes as an assortment of doctors poked and probed every orifice, looking for god knows what, and asking inane questions that would have embarrassed the most seasoned barmaids. "Are you...? Do you...? Can you...?"

And while all of this was going on, imagine, if you will, the scene. We were asked to disrobe completely, taking off everything but our shoes and socks. Having done so, we then passed alongside an assortment of doctors, carrying all of our clothes on one arm while holding in our other hand the forms for the doctors to fill out.

"Bend over. That's fine. Cough! Good, you'll do just fine. Say 'Aaah'. Do you like girls? Are you crazy?"

When all this insanity was completed, we were invited to put on our clothes and wait. If we had passed the final physical, we were to be interviewed by representatives of the different branches of the service. After my interview, I was offered enlistment in the marines or the navy. I didn't care for the prospect of storming countless Pacific beaches, even with John Wayne at my side, and neither did I cherish the idea of hanging over the rail of a ship, being seasick for days, So I chose neither. Luckily, since those branches of the military had reached their quota early that morning, I was allowed to join the army. I was officially inducted on that day, November 2, 1943, and was given a three-week furlough at home before being assigned to an undivulged Army base.

Since I was only the second member of my extended family to enter active military service, I became an instant adult, worthy of respect. The three weeks, filled with expensive dinners, Broadway plays, and family visits, raced quickly by. When my mother woke me on November 23, 1943, at 4:30 a.m., I dressed quietly, packed a small suitcase, and sat down to the last breakfast I was to have at home for the foreseeable future. She handed me a small parcel of food, saying, "Just in case they forget to feed you lunch."

My mother refused to go with my father and me to the draft board building, so we said our painful good-byes at home. I assured her that I would take good care of myself and write often.

My father and I drove the three miles in silence. When we arrived, he parked the car and we got out. We stood outside the building, thinking of last-minute things to say. We both felt the anguish of my uncertain future. We embraced. I told him to say hello to all our relatives and friends. Not knowing what else to say, and finding the moment difficult, I simply assured him, as I had my mother, that I would write often. I told him to take care of himself and the family. We said one last good-bye. I turned and walked away without looking back, entered the building, and began a new life that would change me forever, if I were lucky enough to survive the experience.

PART EIGHT

Falling in Love

Itz and Estelle dancing at Danny and Michele's wedding

Itz and his family in the 1970s

This is Your Life, Estelle Wyetzner   19

Itzik

I first met Estelle Wyetzner when she was eighteen years old. I had arranged to meet my cousin Molly at NYU so that we could go shopping together, something we did with frightening regularity. As I stood at the Chock full o' Nuts store across from NYU, on University Place, waiting impatiently, I noticed Molly approaching. She was talking to a young woman as she walked toward me. "Estelle, this is my cousin, Irving Glasser. Itz, this is Estelle Wyetzner." We were introduced formally, and as I surreptitiously looked her over, I remember thinking, "This is my dream girl." Estelle was buxom, with a swarthy, Mediterranean complexion and long, black hair.

We made small talk as we walked Estelle to the subway station. And as we said good-bye, I knew once again that Molly had started something that I couldn't finish.

While we were making our way to the local men's shop, I said, "Molly, she seems very nice. Tell me about her." Molly's curt answer: "Forget it, she has a boyfriend." So I forgot it. And our conversation turned to other important matters. "Molly," I said, "does a paisley tie look okay with a plaid shirt, multicolored pants, and a bright red jacket for dinnerware?" "Yes," Molly answered, "if the party is being held at the circus." My taste at the time was not very well developed.

Anyway, several weeks went by and the next time I saw Molly, she said, "Do you remember that girl I introduced you to at NYU?"

I remembered, and I said, "Yes." Molly said, "Well, she's broken up with her boyfriend, so if you're interested, why don't you give her a call?" I called Estelle and she was very responsive, as I knew she would be. She said, "Where do I know you from?" Well, I spent about twenty minutes trying to get her to remember anything about me, without success. Finally, she said, "Yes, I remember you. Very tall, dark hair, and a handlebar mustache?" I figured that that was what she wanted, so I said, "Yes." Now Molly must have really touted me, because this kid told me about a daylong NYU boat ride up the Hudson River to a picnic area, and she invited me to be her date. I accepted and we made all the necessary arrangements. Little did I know that the boat ride would be my undoing.

Two weeks later, on a Saturday morning, I arrived at Estelle's house at seven a.m. She had packed us a generous lunch and together we started off to meet Molly and Steve at the boat in Manhattan. The long boat ride was very pleasant and afforded us the opportunity to tell lots of little lies about ourselves. I found Estelle charming, delightful, intelligent, generous, well-educated, wealthy, and an all-around wonderful person and a Girl Scout ... but I wasn't prepared. It was a bright, sunny day, and in the early evening, as the boat made its return trip to New York, I felt that I didn't want the day to end.

Molly and Steve had decided to go to the famous Turnpike Deli on Queens Boulevard to have dinner. I invited Estelle to join us, and she agreed. After all, it was only six thirty and I guess she, too, wanted the day to last a little bit longer. After dinner, we walked down the street to Addie Vallins, another landmark of the times, for its incomparable ice cream and apple pie desserts. I remember it all as if it were yesterday. It was now about eight thirty, and Estelle decided it was time to start for home. The four of us got into my father's car—I had borrowed it for the day—and began on our way to Jackson Heights. On the way, Molly suggested that we stop and walk around Kissena Park. It was Saturday night, 1951, eight thirty p.m., it was safe to be out. What the hell. I parked the car, and we got out and began walking and talking. I was having a great time. I remember wanting the day to last just a little bit longer, and I guess Estelle felt the same way.

What seemed like moments later, I looked at my watch. It was twelve thirty a.m. We were both shocked. I said, "I'd better get you home." Estelle agreed. I drove her to Jackson Heights quickly, said a hasty good-night, promising to call her soon, and drove off.

The next morning, Estelle called me. She sounded very upset. Her mother, she said, had apparently waited up for her. "What kind of a boy picks up a girl at seven in the morning and brings her back at one o'clock the next day?" her mother had asked her, and added, "I forbid you to ever see him again." After that unforgettably wonderful day, the news hit me like a thunderbolt. I was devastated.

I never saw Estelle again. For years afterward, the words of a famous poet raced through my mind from time to time: "Of all sad words of tongue or pen, the saddest are these: it might have been." But, thinking back, I remember that she wanted six children; I wanted two. She loved the excitement of the city; I preferred the quiet of the country. She wanted a dog; I hated pets. She wanted to work; I didn't. She believed in clean; I believed in neat. You know, we really had very little in common. Nah, it wouldn't have worked out.

Fay and Terry

Kissing Again   20

Mickey

My sister Fay and I have always had a wonderfully close relationship. To this day, Fay likes to recount the story of carrying me around wherever she went. She was thirteen years old when I was born, tall for her age, and wore her hair in a bun that made her look older. As a result, I was often taken for her son. That was fine with her, she said. She claims that I was a very beautiful child, and I never argued with that assessment.

Fay was very attractive, and our uncle Dave urged her to seek a wealthy suitor and husband, one who could provide her with the finer things in life. Fay was not moved by such advice. She thought Terry had many things going for him, even though he did not have much money. You know that when someone tells you that she loves the special aroma of her boyfriend that she is truly smitten. Years later, Fay realized that the smell she loved so much came from Ivory soap, but by that time she and Terry were long married. Of course she insisted that she always loved Terry's intelligence and high ethical standards most of all, but I knew even as a child then that their love affair would last for a lifetime. As a seven year old, I thoroughly enjoyed the times when Terry came to visit. My brother Itz felt compelled to warn Terry about the monster he loved so much, but I preferred following the young lovebirds around. I would announce to the world that there they were, "kissing again." Fortunately, they thought I was cute and didn't take umbrage at my intrusion. Seventy years later, at his ninetieth birthday party, Terry recounted the story of my repeated public declaration of their display of affection.

Terry thought Fay was absolutely beautiful. When one of his relatives commented that Fay had very small breasts, Terry was undaunted. "Don't worry," he quipped, "I have very small hands." The years passed; Fay and Terry married and later had two delightful children—David and Ellen—and I would often visit them with my family. One evening, when I was seventeen, Fay invited me for dinner alone, just before I was to leave for summer work at the Evergreen Manor in the Catskill Mountains. I was very impressed, for Fay had never asked me to dinner except in the company of my siblings and parents. I soon found out that there was an agenda for the evening.

Several years earlier, Fay had taken it upon herself to talk to me about "the birds and the bees." This time she had a different story to tell. She wanted to warn her young and naïve brother about the dangers that lay before him.

Fay advised me that some women in the Catskills were there for a month or more, and their husbands visited only on the weekends. While most of these women were probably loyal to their marriages, there were always a few, she continued, who were looking for a brief summer "fling." Fay warned me not to become involved with any of them. "It will do you no good and can spoil you for a more appropriate relationship," she insisted. I listened attentively and promised to be faithful to her values and mine.

At the end of the summer I had a few things to tell Fay and Terry, and I invited myself to their apartment to complete the conversation. When Fay asked me how the summer had gone, I told her that I was very disappointed. Despite her having raised my expectations by detailing the dangers that lurked before me, not one woman of any age approached me. True there seemed to be some affairs going on between staff and guests, but I was never included. All those so-called bored women regarded me as a cute younger brother and never dreamed of any dalliance such as the one that Fay had outlined. My sister just laughed at my complaints and congratulated me. "Obviously, my advice worked. You took everything I said to heart, so you didn't give off any signals that you were available." I was never totally convinced that the problem lay in my not giving off appropriate signals.

Terry and I were very close over the years. I remember how pleased I was when he took me to several Giants football games, where we devoured tuna fish sandwiches that Fay had prepared for us. Since I was a notoriously poor eater, my enjoyment of the sandwiches seemed even more important than my excitement about the game. Sometimes Terry joined Itz and me for our famous punchball games, and it was always fun to be with him. Terry was about fifteen years older than I and knew so much. I learned a lot from him, including some new ideas about religious philosophy. Terry always prided himself on his devout atheism. His yeshiva education notwithstanding, he was not fooled by the presence of any god who could intervene in his life. He had absolute proof: When he was a young boy in the 1930s, he was an avid Giants baseball fan. The Giants had been locked in a tight race for the pennant with their nemesis, the St. Louis Cardinals. Before one crucial game, Terry prayed with all his might that God should see to it that the Giants would win. Suddenly he was struck by the realization that there were equally passionate young kids praying to God for a Cardinals victory. Obviously, God could not make everyone happy—no matter how devout the prayers. "At that moment," he declared with self-satisfaction, "I gave up my belief in God forever."

Fast-forward about forty years, to 1978, when Fay and Terry were visiting my family in Northampton. Josh was ten years old and already a rabid Red Sox fan. Here were the Red Sox locked into a pennant race with the dreaded New York Yankees, and the whole thing came down to one playoff game. Terry adored Josh and wanted him to be happy. "God," he said, "I am giving you one more chance.

If the Red Sox win, I'll reconsider our relationship. If not, it is curtains between us." Suffice it to say Terry remained an undying atheist, but Josh has always loved Uncle Terry for the gamble he made on his nephew's behalf.

There was one other encounter between Terry and the Almighty that had taken place a decade earlier. Terry, Fay, their daughter Ellen, Penina, and I made a cross-country trip together. None of us had ever been out West before, and we proposed this wonderful adventure to them. Terry always regarded such suggestions as preposterous, and his immediate answer was "No! I am not going!" Fay, undaunted, simply began making plans with us—where we would go, what parks we would visit, et cetera. One day we arrived at their apartment, and Terry casually commented about one place in the West that he hoped we could all see. Aha! Faced with the reality that Fay really intended to go without him, he had changed his mind.

The trip was a great success. One glorious evening we drove to the rim of the Grand Canyon. It was an unusual approach, and when we arrived at Lipan Point at sunset, no one else was there. The canyon, bathed in the waning sunlight, overwhelmed us with its size and grandeur. "See," Terry the atheist told us, "that is God saying 'This is what I can do if I want to. You are just lucky I don't want to more often.'" The rest of us were silent.

Our families remained close from the moment I married until the present day. When I first brought Penina to meet Fay and Terry I explained to her that not only were they intelligent and lovely people, but also that my sister Fay was an immaculate housekeeper. "You will find their apartment to be fastidiously clean," I emphasized. On one of those early visits, Fay showed Penina how she washed the curtains every single week. Penina was young and influenced by the early stages of the women's movement. "You cannot waste all your talent and intelligence on washing curtains," she exclaimed. "You have to have a career." Fay took all this to heart and began her reentry into the world of work. She went on to become an extraordinary fifth-grade teacher, much feared and beloved by generations of students in Bedford Stuyvesant, a poor, mostly black neighborhood where students benefited from her determination that they would learn in her class. Years later, Penina tried to claim 10 percent of Fay's pension, arguing that she deserved a commission for urging Fay to give up housecleaning for a "real" profession. Fay and Terry were always generous to us, but somehow the pension argument didn't fly, despite the fact that Terry served as Penina's attorney.

But we were paid in many other ways. When I was writing my dissertation, I asked Terry whether he would be willing to read the chapters and do some light editing. Little did I know that this would become a second career for him. Forget the light editing; he read every word scrupulously, checking everything from commas to overuse of jargon. Until this day, the four of us can recount the time that, to Terry's chagrin, he found the word "evaluate" used five times on one page. This was indeed a cardinal sin. Within an hour we had altered the word four times. Instead of evaluate, we substituted "assess," "judge," "appraise," and "weigh." Penina and I spent many weekends at their apartment, editing in pre-computer style by cutting and pasting and crossing out. Scraps of paper littered Fay's shiny floors, but she never said a word until the day's work was done, and we could sweep up the detritus. The next morning we would awaken to a breakfast of cottage cheese and jam on toast, and the process would begin all over again.

Finally the thesis was done, and I received my Ph.D. You might think that Fay and Terry were then allowed to have their weekends back, but this was not to be. Soon after, Penina began work on her dissertation, and we resumed our working weekends at the Lichtash home. Only this time, we came with a baby. Now Fay helped take care of Josh in addition to everything else. One day Penina became exhausted as Terry and I reread one of her chapters for the umpteenth time. "Please," we said, "you are holding us back. Go out with Fay and Josh so we can work in peace." They went out for a couple of hours, and we continued our hunt for better word choices and exacting punctuation.

For years after that, Penina and I never submitted a manuscript for publication until Terry had read it to ensure that there were no rough edges. Several copy editors commented that our manuscripts were amazingly clean. One of those editors wrote that he thought he had died and gone to heaven when he began working on our book. We were not surprised by his sentiment, because we had been served over the years by our own guardian angels.

The love affair between our families has continued over the generations. Josh and his family try to visit Fay and Terry whenever they are in New York. We all enjoy watching Fay, Ellen, and our granddaughter Einav sit around discussing the ways of the world as if they were old friends. And in some ways they are.

Penina at her wedding in 1960

Mickey and Penina

The Girl with the Funny Name

21

Mickey

I never gave serious consideration to marrying someone who wasn't Jewish. I had grown up in a Jewish world, surrounded by family and Jewish neighbors. I even attended The City College of New York, which was predominantly Jewish. I never had to face the question of dating a non-Jewish woman, yet I did know that my cousin Bert had gone to the University of Michigan as an undergraduate and had married his girlfriend Toni, despite the pleas of his father, my Uncle Dave, to reconsider. I had heard the hushed stories that were circulating in the extended family. At about the same time, I left Brooklyn for graduate school in Cleveland. There, for the first time, I met interesting non-Jewish women I could date. Could it become anything more serious? Truthfully, I simply wasn't sure.

But fate intervened through a brief conversation I had with my mother early one morning when I was home on vacation. My mother was up early as usual, squeezing fresh orange juice, poaching eggs, and making toast. The kitchen was warm, and the food smelled good; it was wonderful to be home. On this day my mother seemed particularly distracted. I remember bending over, tying my shoelaces on the hot radiator, as I was thinking about the things I had to do that day. It was vacation, but I had calls to make and papers to write. In a split second, the silence would be broken by the simple words of my mother, who made it a principle never to interfere in the lives of her children. But this day was different. It was a small plea to her youngest child, the one named after her beloved father. She looked at me directly and said, "Don't break our hearts by marrying a Gentile girl." I didn't move, I didn't respond. She did not say another word; she didn't have to.

The conversation ended that quickly. My mother Ida had come to America from Russia in 1912. She was twelve years old, the second-oldest child, and the oldest of four sisters. Almost immediately, she went to work in a factory and, as a result, she had very little literacy in either Yiddish or English. All her life she suffered from this lack of reading and writing skills. She revered education and encouraged her children to pursue learning in every way possible. Her message always included the requirement that her children lead *edel* and gentle lives in relating to others. In my eyes, she was a model of her own high standards. In later years, my cousin Mollie confirmed this. She said that her mother Bessie was the neediest of the four sisters, and my mother was the most compassionate and supportive. I never wanted to disappoint her.

A year after my mother admonished me not to break her heart, I left Cleveland and continued my studies at Rutgers University in New Jersey. The master's program in sociology, in which I was enrolled, included a theory seminar for first-year graduate students and Douglass college seniors. Liz Enright, one of the seniors, was a smart and insightful woman; we became good friends. She liked me and alerted one of her friends, Penina, about me, this cute graduate student. "He's not religious enough for me, but he's just right for you," she told her friend.

Unbeknownst to me, she told Penina that the seminar had a coffee break every Thursday at 4:30. "Why don't you come over to the student center at that time, and I'll introduce you?" And so we met. When I saw Penina again at a Hillel dance a couple of weeks later, I had forgotten her name and was embarrassed when she danced by me and greeted me warmly. The next time I saw Liz, I rather sheepishly asked her to remind me of her friend's name—"you know, the girl with the funny name." Liz urged me to call her, saying, "she's very nice."

Back in my mother's kitchen a few weeks later, I told her that I had met a particularly nice girl at Rutgers—someone I wanted her to meet. "I think you would really like her. Her name is Penina." My mother said nothing for a few minutes. I was a little perplexed by her reaction. Only later did she ask, "Penina? What kind of a name is Penina?" Neither she nor I knew that it was a Hebrew name. In the years to follow she would come to know the name and love the woman.

PART NINE

In Memoriam

Yudis and Sid

My Sister, My Teacher Sarah (Yudis) Weiner (1922–2013)

22

Mickey

Picture this scene—it was October 1, 1934. My mother, Ida, was about to give birth at home, in a cold-water flat in Brooklyn. Fortunately, it was a mild day in the fall. I say fortunate because our four-room apartment had no central heating—just a large, iron stove in the kitchen. There was no regular doctor in attendance. An arrangement had been made for a doctor to arrive as the labor neared its end—hopefully, just in time for the actual delivery. That limited the expense in the midst of the Great Depression.

The Glazers' second daughter, Yudis, then twelve years old, skipped school to assist her mother in the birth. All went according to some divine plan, and the baby boy was born. Me. Yudis, as she told me repeatedly over the years, immediately fell in love with me. In her eyes, I was perfect. For one thing, I could challenge my brother's position as the only son—the favored child—in the family, and that gave her great satisfaction. From the first day of my life onward, my sister showered me with unlimited love and appreciation, praising any success I had.

She even served as my protector in the semi-tough Brownsville neighborhood. She let the word go out to friend and foe alike: Keep your hands off Mickey Glazer lest you incur the wrath of not only his big brother (which would have been scary enough), but also of his sister Yudis, who was as tough as any two bullies.

Lest you get the wrong idea that Yudis was all physical brawn, let me correct your impression. Her influence on me also extended to matters of the brain and the feet. She literally affected me from head to toe. When I was about fifteen years old, she was the one who introduced me to foreign films at the nearby Hopkinson Theatre, where we saw some of the great Italian and French post-war films. We both were taken with the film Harvest, and Yudis helped me appreciate the characters who were portrayed as ordinary farm people, unlike the Hollywood celebrities of the day. She pointed out how warmth, compassion, and devotion between the characters could blossom into love. She wanted me to know that a man could be gentle and still tough enough to get on in the world. In later years, whenever I was complimented on my good manners in a world that often neglected civil behavior, I could always boast that I was the fortunate beneficiary of growing up with two older sisters.

Yudis was also determined that I overcome my natural shyness on the dance floor. Despite my resistance, she pressured me into taking dancing lessons—taught by her, of course. She paid me the ultimate compliment after several weeks, when she proclaimed that I was now ready to dance with any girl without embarrassing myself or her.

Of course, Yudis's accomplishments went far beyond our relationship and her role as my teacher. She was deeply involved with and proud of her children, grandchildren, great-grandchild, and many others around her. Beyond family, she was also the public-spirited citizen who, with a friend, collected empty soda cans on the street and donated the refunded deposits to a variety of charities. Yudis embraced life, whether collecting cans, helping out at the Brooklyn Senior Center, or singing in the chorus. She did it with enthusiasm and affection that all of us will always cherish.

When family and friends remember Yudis, most of all they will recall gathering around her small dining room table to partake of all the foods she prepared. There was never enough room, so we ate in shifts or sat on the couch. We didn't care, as long as she served her classic dishes—pickled salmon, rice pudding, sautéed mushrooms, and more. But the ultimate treat was dessert—sampling Yudis's extraordinary cookies. They were plain sugar cookies that melted in your mouth, and there were always extras stashed away for us to take home. We'll never forget them, and they can become part of your life too. When I think of my sister, it is not with a tear. It is with a smile, with pride, and with joyful memories.

Yudis's Cookies

6 eggs, separated
2 c. sugar
2 c. shortening (Yudis used Crisco)
1 c. orange juice
6 c. flour (approximate)
3 tsp. baking powder
pinch of salt
2 tsp. vanilla

Beat egg whites, adding sugar until it forms a soft meringue.

Make a well in the egg white mixture and add shortening, egg yolks, juice, and vanilla.

Mix lightly with electric mixer.

Add baking powder and salt to flour and add flour slowly to batter until dough is firm.

Add remaining flour by hand until dough is thick enough to roll.

Dough can be refrigerated.

Roll out dough and cut cookies with cookie cutter or top of a glass.

Decorate with poppy seeds (optional).

Bake at 375 degrees until lightly browned.

Don't eat too many at one time!

Marcy and Joel in 1965

Summer of 1967
Marcy Migdal (1947-2013) 23

Mickey

Recently, Penina and I were heading to Amherst, a town a half-hour's drive away, for a 3:00 p.m. doctor's appointment. Despite some traffic, we arrived at exactly 2:59. To my surprise, there was a long line of patients ahead of me waiting to check in, so I stood patiently for ten minutes or so. The clerk told me to be seated until she called me. Several minutes later, by now about 3:20, the receptionist told me that since I had arrived fifteen minutes late for my appointment, the doctor refused to see me, and I would have to reschedule. Normally, I am not confrontational in situations like this, but this was outrageous. I spoke up and firmly told her that I had driven a half-hour and had indeed arrived in time, only to wait more than ten minutes on line. I was in no mood to reschedule. My protest led to a reconsideration, and the doctor came in apologetically soon after.

The entire episode, as inconsequential as it seems, took me in a flash to a scene many years earlier, in the summer of 1967. The place was Harvard Square, and the cast of characters included Marcy, Joel, Penina, me, and a friend from England. We had all organized our work schedules to meet for a 3:00 p.m. showing of The War Game, an important film about nuclear holocaust. As our group arrived, I went into the lobby to buy five tickets, only to be told by the cashier that she would not sell me tickets because we had arrived three minutes after the 3:00 deadline. Given the nature of the opening scene, the theater would not admit any latecomers. Rather deflated, I went out to tell the others that our plans were foiled. We were all very disappointed except for Marcy. This twenty-year-old whippersnapper looked me straight in the eye and, without hesitation, said, "You go right back in there and demand that she sell us the tickets. The movie hasn't started yet, and it is a stupid policy." With Marcy's vehemence at my back, I returned to the cashier and demanded that she sell us the tickets. Seeing my determination (or Marcy's), she relented, and we all felt it was a small victory for common sense. You can see why, all these years later, I felt Marcy sitting on my shoulder when I confronted the doctor's office and refused to reschedule my appointment.

Lots of other good things happened in Boston that summer. For one thing, the city was consumed with baseball fever. After years of dismal records, the Boston Red Sox had come alive and were battling for a first-place finish in the American League. The four of us had been Yankees, Dodgers, or Phillies fans who had sort of lost interest in baseball, but no one could resist the pennant fever that permeated the city. We went to our first game in Fenway Park, and all of us became Red Sox fans, at least for that time. Some of us never got over it.

That summer we even developed our own family jokes. A friend had brought us a gift of babas au rum from the gourmet shop, Cardullo's, on Harvard Square. We opened the jar very expectantly, since they were a lot fancier than any dessert we could afford to buy and none of us had ever eaten them before. Instead of soft, delicate cakes marinated in a rum sauce, we were very disappointed by hard little lumps of dough that had failed to rise. Everyone agreed that Penina should return the jar and tell Cardullo's that something was wrong. Well—a very snooty sales person listened to the complaint and then said, condescendingly, " Obviously, you know nothing about babas." Penina creatively replied that she had tasted them many times and these were bad. She finally got a refund. Nobody was happier than

Marcy, whose love of justice was only superseded by her intolerance for stupidity. For years after, when someone was insulting or arrogant, we would say to each other, "Obviously, they know nothing about babas."

The summer of '67 was wonderful for all of us. Joel, not yet enrolled in graduate school, was assisting me on a research project at Harvard. Penina was pregnant with Josh and working on her dissertation, and Marcy had a part-time job and was planning her senior thesis. We were house-sitting in a big, beautiful place in the heart of Cambridge and thoroughly enjoying the whole scene. The four of us took many evening walks and stopped to watch the neighborhood softball teams play; we went to the beach, and we "drank in" Boston and Cambridge. For Joel and Marcy it was a very romantic time, just before they got engaged—and the beginning of a lifelong love affair.

Itz and Danny

Apropos of Nothing: an Appreciation

24

Danny Glasser

I was well into my teens when I discovered my father's hidden past. One evening, in the basement of our Brooklyn home, my father and my older brother opened a box of aging papers marked "PERETZ FAMILY CIRCLE" and began to read aloud. During the late 1940s and early 1950s, my father had been the author of a newsletter about and for his extended family's regular gatherings, at that time mostly first-generation Jewish immigrants in their forties and fifties and their children. I don't remember many specifics of the stories—just some digs about an older relative's poor personal hygiene—but I do remember literally rolling on the floor laughing so hard that my jaw ached.

In the late 1940s my father was in his early twenties, a high school graduate (barely), and a veteran of World War II. He had yet to meet the woman who would become his wife of forty years, my mother. And he was trying to make a go as a comedy writer. Humor was for him a salve against the sadness, tedium, and low-grade insanity of ordinary life; it was also something of a calling. He used to tell a story about when he was in the army and won second prize in a talent show for his act, telling jokes. First prize, he said, had been won by a man who simply walked across the stage dressed in drag. Eventually, as my father's life became filled with the milestones of adulthood—marriage, children, a hard-earned college degree, a fitful career, home ownership—his dreams of being a professional comedian and writer were packed away like so many typewritten pages in a box. But he never stopped telling stories and trying to make people laugh.

His impish wit occasionally got him into trouble. One of many examples—and my personal favorite—concerned a time when he worked in a record store. [Attention: If you are below the age of thirty, ask your parents what a "record store" was.] A customer came into the store and asked for a copy of Beethoven's Fifth Symphony. My father cracked wise, "Do you want Ludwig van Beethoven or Harold Beethoven?," expecting a chuckle in response. The customer's face turned pale. "I don't know," he said, "I'm getting it as a gift for a friend, and he didn't specify." My father thought for a moment and replied, "I'll tell you what. Most people prefer the Ludwig van Beethoven. Why don't you take that, and if it turns out it's the wrong Beethoven, you can bring it back and I'll exchange it." The customer pointed to a sign on the wall. "It says 'Absolutely No Returns or Exchanges.'" My father replied, "Don't worry, I'll remember you, and in this case I'll make an exception."

As children, my brother, sister, and I loved listening to our father's stories and improvisations, mostly because they made us laugh. We inherited and shared his love of the Marx Brothers, early stand-up comedians such as Bill Cosby, and, later, the television show Monty Python's Flying Circus. Through all of this, we absorbed his philosophy that nothing in life should be taken too seriously and that any disappointment or failure would eventually be eased by mining it for its humor.

"Apropos of nothing..." This was often how my father started telling a story. Partly a verbal throat clearing, partly a call to attention, it signaled that we were about to hear about the world from his own, slightly twisted point of view. As he got older and his family nest emptied, he rediscovered writing and storytelling, this time with the benefit of a more mature and bittersweet perspective. He told his stories at numerous family *simchas*—celebrations—and the reconstituted Peretz Family Circle reunions, introducing younger generations to the then-mostly gone first generation and reminding the then-aging second generation of their youthful misdeeds. "The good old days—they were terrible," he liked to remark. His growing body of work was cut short by his untimely death twenty years ago.

One of our last in-person conversations occurred on the weekend of my thirtieth birthday. My father showed me the draft of a story he had written for the occasion. It was about an accident I'd had when I was three years old, an accident for which he had always felt responsible but that I had long ago put in the past. I read the story as if he wanted editorial feedback and responded as such; it quickly became apparent that he had written the story as a birthday gift and as an apology. I had become enough of an adult to appreciate that my father's stories were for him equal parts legacy and therapy.

My father didn't live to see his grandchildren, to attend all of his children's weddings, or to share his retirement with my mother. He didn't get his long-sought little convertible with (of course) a stick shift. He never got to blog, to tweet, or to see his stories published. I have an audio recording of my father reading his story "Chocolate Pudding"; it's one of the very few times my children have heard the sound of his voice. I hope this book brings them closer to their grandfather, his family, and his life.

Daniel "39 Arrests Without a Conviction" Glasser
August 2014

Acknowledgments

First and foremost I thank Itz's family for giving me the honor of collecting and publishing his stories. The family has been supportive and helpful throughout the process. His children, Paul, Ruth, and Danny edited his stories; Paul and Danny wrote meaningful introductory and concluding essays; Estelle helped us with photos and encouragement. Other family, Fay and Terry Lichtash, David Lichtash, Ellen Jones, and Jerry Siegel contributed photos and memories of earlier times. I thank my son Josh for his touching and insightful essay.

I never would have started writing short stories about my life if my wife had not insisted that I try Dorothy Goldstone's memoir writing workshop at our synagogue, Congregation B'nai Israel. Dorothy's approach and the support from other workshop members convinced me to continue writing. A few months later, I enrolled in the Learning in Retirement memoir writing seminar led by Henny Lewin and Steffi Schamess. There I joined a dozen other writers who read and commented on each other's work. It was a rewarding experience.

Many family and friends graciously listened to my stories as I completed them. They usually laughed in the right places and sighed where it was appropriate. Some like Herman Teitelbaum, Miriam and Paul Slater, Michael Lewis, Ayala Rosen, Tamar Noam Glazer, Joshua Glazer, and Einav Glazer offered helpful comments that improved some of my early drafts.

Jean Zimmer was an excellent editor, combining her skills and knowledge of the Chicago Manual of Style with good humor and positive support. Steve Strimer once again proved that he is a creative and knowledgeable publisher who has devoted time and energy to helping local authors.

All the clichés that authors write about the indispensable help of their partners turns out to be true in this case. For all this I thank my wife Penina.

About the Authors

Irving Martin Glasser (1925–1994), affectionately known as Itz or Itzik to his family, was born in the Brownsville section of Brooklyn. He completed elementary and high school during the Great Depression of the 1930s and then served for three years in New Guinea, the Philippines, and Japan in the U.S. Army during World War II. He returned home, used the GI Bill to attend Brooklyn College, and worked in various retail businesses, while writing comedy for the enjoyment of family and friends. He lived in Brooklyn with his wife Estelle and their three children for the rest of his life.

Myron (Mickey) Glazer, Itz's younger brother, grew up in Brooklyn, enjoying his older siblings, extended family, and the friends in his East New York neighborhood. After graduating from City College, he left Brooklyn at age twenty-one to attend graduate school. Although he never lived there again, he regularly visited family and friends in Brooklyn. After schooling in Cleveland, Ohio and New Brunswick and Princeton, New Jersey, Mickey lived with his wife and their two children in Northampton, Massachusetts, where he taught at Smith College for forty-one years. He has cowritten several books with his wife Penina, including *The Whistleblowers: Exposing Corruption in Government and Industry*; *The Environmental Crusaders: Confronting Disaster and Organizing Community*; and *The Jews of Paradise: Creating a Vibrant Community in Northampton, Massachusetts*.

Our Legacy

Itz's grandchildren – Golda, Anna, Alexancer, Leah, and Isaac

Mickey's grandchildren – Idan, Natan, Einav, and Justin